Contents

Practical Household Hints

Handy tables

Still got some old knitting needles and crochet hooks in your workbag and confused about what the metric equivalent is? Unsure what the gas equivalent of 250°C is? Worry not. All the information you need is on the following pages.

Practical Household Hints

Useful Tips for Homeowners

Michael Johnstone

Capella

This edition printed 2004

For: Bookmart Limited
Registered Number 2372865
Trading as Bookmart Limited
Blaby Road, Wigston, Leicester LE18 4SE

Revised edition of title published as
'*1001 Household Hints and Tips*'.

Cover design by Alex Ingr
Text design by Chris Smith

© Arcturus Publishing Limited, 2002
Unit 26/27 Bickels Yard, 151-153 Bermondsey Street
London SE1 3HA

ISBN 1-84193-255-8

Printed and bound in China

Knitting needles

Old Size	New Size
000	10
00	9
0	8
1	7.5
2	7
3	6.5
4	6
5	5.5
6	5

Knitting needles

Old Size	New Size
7	4.5
8	4
9	3.75
10	3.25
11	3
12	2.75
13	2.25
14	2

Crochet hooks for wool

2	7mm
3	6mm
4	6mm
5	5.5mm
6	5mm
7	4.5mm
8	4mm
9	3.5mm
10	3.25mm
11	3mm
12	2.75mm
13	2.25mm
14	2mm

Crochet hooks for cotton

1.5	2mm
2.5	1.75mm
3.5	1.5mm
4.5	1.25mm
5.5	1.00mm
6.5	0.75mm
7	0.60mm

Collar sizes

Inches	14.5	15	15.5	16	16.5	17	17.5
Centimetres	37	38	39/40	41	42	43	44

Waist measurements

Inches	26	28	30	32	34	36	38	40	42
Centimetres	66	71	76	81	86	91	97	102	107

Shoe sizes

(These can differ just a little from make to make, which is why, for European sizes, we have given two equivalents – try both on and select the one that fits best. And when buying shoes, women should always be wearing tights, and men the weight of socks they usually wear.)

British	3	4	5	6	7	8	9	10	11
Europe	36/37	37/38	38/39	39/40	40/41	42/43	43/44	44/45	45/46
USA		4.5/45	5.5/55	6.5/65	7.5/75	8.5/85	9.5/95		

Women's clothing

Size	inches bust/hip	cm bust/hip
8	30/32	76/81
10	32/34	81/86
12	34/36	86/91
14	36/38	91/97
16	38/40	97/102
18	40/42	102/107
20	42/44	107/112
22	44/46	112/117
24	46/48	117/122

Roughly speaking

1oz = 25g   1/4pint =150ml   1/4 teaspoon = 1.25ml
2oz = 50g   1/2pint = 300ml   1/2 teaspoon = 2.5ml
3oz = 75g   1 pint = 600ml   1 teaspoon = 5ml
4oz = 100g   2 pints = 120ml   1 tablespoon = 15ml
8oz = 200g

Oven temperatures

Centigrade	Fahrenheit	Gas mark
100 very cool	200	Low
110 very cool	225	1/4
120 very cool	250	1/2
140 cool	275	1
150 cool	300	2
160 cool	325	3
180 moderate	350	4
190 moderate hot	375	5
200 moderate hot	400	6
220 hot	425	7
230 hot	450	8
240 very hot	475	9
260 very hot	500	10

Practical Household Hints

Around the house

Hanging pictures? Got frozen pipes? Bathroom mirrors keep steaming up? Tips on how to cope with these and a host of other problems are here for your perusal.

After the party

Always clear up as much as you can before you go to bed after hosting a party. Put everything in the kitchen, empty the dregs from glasses down the sink and leave them to soak overnight, scrape leftovers from plates into a big, black polythene bag, and stack the plates. Empty the ashtrays, open a window or two for a few minutes and then go to bed. It's a chore, true, but if you don't and you wake up in the morning, even thinking about all these chores is enough to keep you in bed all day!

Ants

If you've got ants coming into your house, try spreading some cinnamon, catnip or chalk wherever you think they're coming in.

Bathroom mirrors

Prevent bathroom mirrors from steaming up by spraying a thin coating of shaving cream onto the dry mirror and rubbing it with lint-free cloth until the cream disappears. You can also stop them fogging up by having lighted candles when you bath or shower or running a couple of centimetres of cold water into the bath before adding the hot.

Audiovisual gear

Don't keep your hi-fi and VCR on the floor, all that stooping is bad for the back. If you can, keep them at waist level, and store your video, CDs etc on a shelf alongside. And remember that an average shelf is deep enough to store them two-deep. Build a raised insert half the width of the shelf so that the ones at the back can be reached easily.

Bath plug

If your bath plug has come off the chain and you put the plug somewhere and can't remember where, use a golf ball until you find it or buy another one. The water pressure keeps it in place and if you kick it out accidentally, it rolls back into place.

Bathroom safety – 1

If you have to have a lock on the bathroom door, install a doorknob with an outside lock release. That way if the children should lock themselves in, or an adult become ill in the bathroom, you will be able to get in.

Bathroom safety – 2

If an elderly parent or relative is coming to live with you, consider fitting grab bars in the bath and shower and next to the toilet. They are a great boon to those who are not as agile as they used to be.

Bathroom safety – 3

Never, ever – repeat, never, ever use anything that has to be plugged into the mains anywhere near a filled bath. Even a hair dryer can be dangerous – and as for an electric fire, don't even think about it.

Bathroom sense

Keep the things you always use – toothbrush, razor and the like – as close to the sink as you can.

Bed linen

When you buy new sheets, as soon as you take them out of the wrapping, mark them all in the corner with an indelible pen – S for single and D for double. It's much easier to pull what you need out of the linen cupboard as and when you need it.

Bin it

Once a year go through your cupboards and wardrobes and put everything you haven't used for the last twelve months in a large cardboard box and store it somewhere it won't get damp. If you haven't used anything in the box in another twelve months you can safely bin what's in it.

Blanket care

There's something soothing about slipping between freshly laundered sheets and tugging a blanket around you as you snuggle down to sleep. But after you have your blankets dry-cleaned, always make sure they are well aired before you use them again. To do this, suspend the blanket between two lines and pull it into shape. When it's well aired, give it a good shake and bring the pile up with a soft brush.

Blocked sinks

Before calling the plumber – and if you are out of spirits of salt – crumble three Alka-Seltzers and put them down the drain followed by a cup of white vinegar. Wait for a few minutes then run the hot water. If you have plastic sink fittings and can unscrew the sump easily, don't forget to put a bowl under it first before setting to work.

Bookmark

Snip the corner off an old envelope and slip it over the corner of your page when you put your book down. It makes a simple, but effective, bookmark.

Brass bedsteads

When buying a solid brass bedstead make sure that what you buy is the real thing by taking a magnet with you. If what you are offered as solid brass is that, the magnet won't be attracted to it. But if the bedstead is metal coated in brass, the magnet will cling to it.

Brass taps

Keep your brass taps clean either by using just a little very mild washing up liquid and rinsing with cold water, or wash them with White Spirit. They also come up a real treat and the shine lasts for ages if you smear them with brown sauce and then buff them with half a lemon dipped in salt. Brass candle sticks and other items will also shine if treated the same way.

Broken light bulbs

First, make sure that the light switch is off. Second, if you don't have a glove to hand, wait a minute or two before changing the bulb – bulbs get very hot. Third, keep a supply of all the light bulbs you use, and mark each one – dining room lamp, overhead bedroom etc. Fourth, if a light bulb breaks when you are changing it, cut a potato in half, press the cut side into the broken glass and the bulb should turn enough for you to change it!

Buying a vacuum cleaner

Next time you buy a vacuum cleaner take some salt or sand with you ask the assistant if you can sprinkle on any carpet and use the demonstration model in the showroom to vacuum it up. If he or she says, 'No!' go somewhere else, and if the cleaner you had in mind doesn't pass the test, buy one that does.

CDs

If any of your CDs are loosing clarity of sound keep them in the freezer overnight. You will be astonished at how clear and clean they sound next time you play them.

Candle drips

If your sconces have overflowed with molten wax and it has run onto an unprotected wooden tabletop, scrape off as much as you can very carefully and rub the remaining wax into the wood with a soft, clean cloth.

Candles

Candles burn for longer if you keep them in the fridge.

Candlesticks

If you pop badly waxed candlesticks in the freezer for an hour or two, the hardened wax is easily peeled off. If you don't have time to do this, hold the candlesticks under very hot running water – remembering to put on rubber gloves, of course – and you should be able to push the offending wax off.

Carpets

Make carpets last longer by turning them round so that they wear evenly. And always save the manufacturer's label from a carpet after you lay it. If there are any problems a few years down the line, knowing the carpets brand name, pattern number and all the other information on the label can save hours of frustrating telephone calls.

Children

Make cleaning fun and a game for your young children – they will love helping you and after they get the hang of it, you will have a great little helper who feels very grown up helping Mummy and Daddy with the chores.

Clogged shower heads

All showerheads become clogged eventually, but if you live in a hard-water area, this will happen more frequently. When it does occur, unscrew the showerhead, take the pieces apart and soak them in a bowl of vinegar for at least twelve hours. Any stubborn sediment can be brushed off. When you reassemble the parts and re-attach the head, the water should run as it did when the shower was new.

Carnations and pinks

These perennial favourites seem to last forever if you put them in lemonade (the real thing, not the diet variety) rather than water. Change it every four or five days (and don't be tempted to drink it).

Chrysanthemums

Plunge the cut ends of the flowers into very hot water for a few seconds and then into cold; they will last for weeks.

Coat hangers

Always hang coat hangers with the hooks pointing away from you. It's much easier to remove several garments at once – or, if you need to in a hurry – all of them at once.

Colour co-ordinating

If you like your furniture to match or tone, base your colour scheme around the carpet. The chances are you will be replacing chairs and the sofa before you have to lay a new carpet.

Conversation charts

Tape a metric conversion chart to the inside of your food cupboards and tape a temperature conversion one close to your cooker. All good cookbooks now give these as part of the recipes, but if you are working from an old favourite, having a conversion chart *in situ* can save you frantically leafing through your other cookbooks trying to find the centigrade equivalent of 300°F.

Creaking doors

Rub all the joints in all the hinges with a lead pencil, swing the door back and forth a few times, repeat the whole process and even the squeakiest doors should stop creaking.

Cupboard sense

Put the things you use most often on shelves that are between knee level and head height. Items you use less regularly can be stored on the higher and lower shelves. And in the kitchen, store cast iron casserole dishes and other heavy items within a foot of your waist level. That way you won't risk injuring your back in by stretching to get a heavy item from high up or low down.

Cut flowers

An aspirin or two and a change of water every four days or so will keep most freshly cut flowers blooming in the vase for at least a week (as long as the flowers are freshly cut). All cut flowers will last longer if there are foxgloves in the arrangement.

Cut your heating bills

Even in the coldest winter if you turn your central heating thermostat down one or two degrees from where you usually have it, the only difference you will notice is that your next quarterly bill will be lower than the corresponding one for the previous year.

Daffodils

Resist the temptation to include other blooms in a vase of daffodils. They will all die sooner rather than later. But if you feel that you have to, soak them for an hour in separate water then re-rinse them. And if you add camphor or charcoal to the water, your daffs will keep their spring-like bloom longer. The same works for other narcissi, too.

Damp books

If a book has got wet ,sprinkle talcum powder or cornflour between the damp pages, and leave it for a few hours; the moisture is absorbed and the book is almost as good as new.

Dishwasher

Keep the inside of your dishwasher absolutely immaculate by filling the detergent container with citric acid (you should be able to buy this from you chemist) and running the machine with no dishes in it. If you can't get citric acid, try squeezing two or three lemons and using the juice.

Drying dogs

If you don't have the time to let your dog dry naturally, you can take the hairdryer to your dog. The noise may scare it and make it hard to keep still: better to use a chamois leather – it's quicker than a towel and keeps the animal's coat nice and soft.

Extra work space

If you have a small kitchen and wish you had more work surface, have a piece of wood cut to fit the top of your sink. When you need that little extra space, simply put it in place.

Fireproof

Buy an A-Z organizer from any high-street stationer and find a fireproof box that it will fit into. Keep not just important documents – birth certificates, passports, insurance policies, spare address book and the like – in it, but photographs and other items of sentimental value. Should there be a fire, vital papers will be intact and you will still have those snaps of loved ones, which are impossible to replace.

Fridge doors

The rubber seal round your fridge door must keep the fridge absolutely airtight if it is to work at optimum efficiency. Test it by closing the door on a five-pound note, leaving a small corner sticking out. Then pull on the note: if it slides out with no resistance, the seal isn't airtight and you should either replace it, or adjust the door hinges.

Frozen pipes

If your pipes are frozen turn the water off at the stopcock immediately and open all the taps, and when you identify the frozen section, use a hair drier set on cool to begin to defrost it. Never use boiling water, propane torches of any kind of naked flame. Excessive heating can cause a pipe to explode.

Furniture care

To protect your furniture, keep it out of direct sunlight, never put it in front of a central heating radiator and as soon as anyone drops anything liable to leave a stain on it, clean up immediately.

Glass cutting

If you are having a piece of glass cut to make a coffee table, take a paper pattern of the exact shape and size you want to the cutter. It will make his task much easier. Ask his advice about what weight of glass to use and when you get it, put a small felt circle of the same colour as the base at each corner and at intervals under the edge. They stop the glass slipping.

Hi-fi wiring

When you are wiring up a hi-fi system, keep all the connecting wires as short as possible and neatly arranged between the various components. Not only does a jungle of wires look untidy, it can cause hum and, also, it makes it easier to check the connections if you have a problem.

High ceilings

If your ceilings are too high to clean safely, lay a slightly damp cloth over a helium balloon and float it upwards until it hits the roof. Simply pull it along by its string and the dirt on the ceiling will come off on the cloth.

Insects

As a general rule, insects don't like lavender and a big bowl of fresh, growing lavender by an open window may stop flies and other unwelcome winged visitors taking advantage of your hospitality.

Ironing

Cotton, net and silky rayon garments should be ironed right side up: polyester can be ironed either side: and all other garments are best ironed inside out. If a steam iron is on and not steaming, turn it off and pull the plug out immediately. The vents are probably clogging up and the iron could be dangerous.

Ivory handles

If you have ivory-handled cutlery (a) never put it in the dishwasher and (b) if the handles have yellowed put them on a sunny window sill for a few hours and the gentle bleaching action of the sun will whiten the ivory.

Jewellery cleaner

Drop two Alka-Seltzers into a glass of water, drop in your jewellery for two minutes and they'll come out like new.

Keys

If your house or car keys seem to be a bit sticky, work a lead pencil all over them and as far into the lock as you can, if this is at all possible. (Do this really gently. If the lead breaks in the lock you're in real trouble!) Now lock the key in and out a few times and next time you come to use it, you should find that the key works a treat.

Keeping bugs at bay

It's impossible to keep your home absolutely bug free, but there are one or two things you can do to keep them to a minimum. If you make sure that you wipe up all crumbs after a meal, clean up pet food as soon as your dog or cat has eaten, cover your dustbin and kitchen rubbish bin and clean your drains regularly, that will keep a lot of them away.

Kitchen cupboards and drawers

Take an hour or two to go through your kitchen cupboards and drawers and get rid of all those ancient, rarely used jars and bottles as well as rthe rusty tin openers and corkscrews.

Large parcels

If you are wrapping a large parcel as a present and it's too large for ordinary wrapping paper, buy a large paper tablecloth and use that instead.

Leaky lavatory

If you think that your stopper-ball or stopper-valve is leaking, put a few drops of food colouring into the tank and if any coloured water comes into the bowl before you next flush, you have a leak.

Lost contact lens

If you lose your contact lens at home, get the vacuum cleaner out, take the brush attachment off and stretch the foot of one leg of a pair of tights over the end and sweep it over the carpet. It should pick up the missing lens and the suction power will keep it firmly against the material. You can also do this if you've lost a small earring or something similar.

Manufacturer's instructions

Keep the instructions for all the electrical goods you buy – television, VCR, stereo, electric kettle even – in the same drawer. If you leave them scattered around the house, the chances are that when you come to need them you will have no idea where they are.

Mattresses – 1

Keep your mattresses clean by regularly running your vacuum cleaner over them, then turning them and vacuuming the other side before putting the undersheet back on. Never fail to use an undersheet or, better still, an underblanket: it protects the mattress from sweat and dirt.

Mattresses – 2

Buy the best mattress you can afford. Your back will thank you. As a rule of thumb, a mattress lasts for about ten years, but if it starts to sag in the middle or shows any other signs of being past its best, think seriously about replacing it. You spend a third of your life in bed – you may as well be comfortable.

Memorabilia

Don't throw away your children's old report cards, school photos and the like. The reports may be awful and the photos ghastly years from now, but your children will appreciate it if you save these mementoes of their schooldays and give them to them as a present when they flee the nest.

A message for the milkman

Don't scribble a note for the milkman and ram it into one of the bottles on the doorstep. It can get wet, blow away or be got at by inquisitive cats. Much better to pop your missive into an old (washed) screw-top jam jar.

Mice

Fill some little tubs with used cat litter and put them around the house. The mice take one sniff, think there's a cat just around the corner and head off somewhere safer. If you see a mouse hole, stuff it with steel wool pads: mice won't chew through them.

Microwavable?

Test if a dish is suitable for microwave cooking by putting it in the oven set at high alongside a glass of water for one minute. If the water is cool and the dish is warm, don't use it in the microwave again. Metal should never be used in a microwave.

Midges

Anyone who has visited Scotland during the midge season knows that if they like you there is nothing you can do; if they don't, you can walk through clouds of them unaffected. A lighted cigarette often does the trick – you don't have to smoke it!

Mirror cleaners

Why not use an air freshener to clean mirrors? It does the job just as well as a supermarket glass-cleaner and smells much better.

Mosquitoes – 1

There are many tips which can be used to prevent you being bitten by mosquitoes: some advocate dabbing lavender essential oil (the only essential oil that can be applied directly on the skin) on the pulse points. Others splash on plain alcohol and let it dry to deter the little biters. A mix of half-pure vanilla and half water is also said to be efficient.

Mosquitoes – 2

Drop a little paraffin into any stagnant water: that's where mosquitoes breed and the paraffin will kill any larvae that may be lurking. Keep them at bay with a lighted cigarette or a couple of candles, as they can't stand smoke. And as they loathe basil, a pot or two in places that you have found them will see them off.

Moths – 1

Never store any natural-fibre garments stained with grease. Nine times out of ten, moths will be sure to find it, lay eggs in it and the larvae will have a feast. If you do find that they have got at your clothes, remove any larvae you can see (check collars and pocket flaps). Before you put the clothes back, clean the drawer with a paraffin rag and line it with newspaper. When the clothes are back in place, sprinkle some Epsom salts among them.

Moths – 2

If you are a knitter and are storing wool for a long time, wind it round a mothball.

Narrow spaces

If you have suitable narrow spaces in your house – between your fridge and the wall for example – think about filling them with roll out cupboards. Simply fit castors, shelves and a handle to a suitable-size old drawer and hey presto – extra, organized, storage space.

Old trunks

An old trunk (if there isn't one in your attic, keep an eye out for one at a car boot sale), nicely cleaned up and with a specially-made glass top doubles up as an attractive coffee table and gives you extra storage space, too, for things you don't use very often but can't throw out. And the space between the glass and the trunk top can be used to display photos, theatre programmes and other bits and pieces of family memorabilia.

Ovens

Keep your oven sweet smelling by baking old lemon and orange rinds in it occasionally at 350°F/170°C/Gas mark 4 for half an hour.

Patio furniture

The best way to clean patio furniture quickly is to use the car wash brush attachment fastened to the hose. Use a cleaner appropriate to the material your furniture is made of and it will come up like new.

Picture hanging

If you have several pictures to hang, see how they relate to one another and how best they will go together by laying them on the floor before you even think about banging a picture hook into the wall. And if you want to see where to hang them on the wall, cut out paper shapes the exact size of each picture and Bluetack them to the wall in likely positions. Now reach for the hammer. And if once they are up, you find that one of them keeps slipping at an angle, wrap some adhesive tape around the centre of the wire.

Plastic bottles

The bottom half of an empty, plastic lemonade bottle makes an ideal container for keeping odds and ends – spare nails, screws, batteries, paper clips etc. And the top end makes a great funnel.

Polishing wood

Always rub in the polish and buff with the grain or pattern of the wood, never against it.

Rats?

Call the health inspector!

Roasting trays

You can easily clean metal roasting trays and similar implements by putting them in a black rubbish bag or bin liner, sprinkling them with an eggcupful of household ammonia, tying up the bag and leaving it out of harm's way overnight. When you take them out in the morning, rinse them in hot water and even burned-on grease will come off.

Rocking chairs

If you have a rocking chair and wooden floors, you have probably found that the rockers have worn the floor. To stop this happening, put a piece of masking tape on both rockers.

Roses

To make roses open out and last for days on end, clip the stalk, make four tiny upward incisions from the bottom of the stalk towards the bloom, and curl the outer layer upwards, taking care to keep it attached to the stalk. Put the roses in warm water and they will open beautifully.

Scratches

Scratches on wood furniture can often be disguised by rubbing just a little iodine on the scratch before polishing it with a good beeswax. If you have scratched a piece of marble, use extra fine steel wool to apply baking soda and water mixed to a paste.

Scorch marks

If you have a scorch mark on your carpet trim it back as far as you can, snip some of the pile from a piece of the carpet that's never seen – under a sofa perhaps – and use rubber cement to fix it to the repair area. Work the tufts upright with a pin and when the cement has dried, use the pin to blend them in with the surrounding pile. It won't stand close investigation, but will be perfectly acceptable to most.

Shoe box

Keep a large box lined with plastic by the back and front doors and insist that your family deposit wet shoes, dirty trainers and the like in them before coming into the house.

Simple when you know how

If you make a point of assigning everything its own place and always making sure you put things where they should be, you will never misplace things.

Speaker wire

To stop people tripping over speaker wire, try stapling the wire to a wall or skirting board.

Spectacles

If like most people you are constantly putting your glasses down and forgetting where you put them, buy several pairs of inexpensive, reading glasses now widely available at high street chain chemist shops. Keep a pair in every room. Don't use them as a long-term replacement for prescription spectacles, but as a short-term solution they won't damage your eyes.

Squeegees

If you use a squeegee to clean your windows and the rubber blade is worn, take it out of the holder and turn it round.

Stained sinks

If you have a grubby porcelain kitchen sink fill it with hot water, add a cupful of washing soda and leave it for two hours. After you drain it, you will find that any stains remaining will wipe away easily.

Sticking doors

Before taking a plane to a door that's been sticking, wait for a spell of cool, dry weather. If a door sticks during warm, sticky weather, it may just be the humidity that's the problem. If it's not that, check that that screws in the hinges and strike plate haven't come loose:

often simply tightening them with a screwdriver is all that's needed. And if you have to plane, never work against the grain.

Street noise

If traffic and other noises disturb you and you don't have or don't want double glazing, try hanging heavier curtains (or simply try hanging curtains if you don't have them).

Stuck drawers

If a drawer becomes stuck or the handle come off and you can't get it back on without opening the drawer, try opening it with a rubber plunger. It should be strong enough to get the drawer open and won't leave a permanent mark on the wood.

Stuck tumblers

If you left tumblers overnight, one inside the other, and they have become attached to each other so strongly they are reluctant to part, fill the top one with cold water and stand the bottom one in warm water. They will soon separate.

Telephone answering machines

Say as little as possible on your outgoing message – just that you can't come to the phone and will return the call as soon as possible. Never say that you're going to be away until a week on Tuesday or whenever – prospective burglars know they have until a week on Monday to get into your house!

Tidy tidying

When the tidying bug strikes and you decide to attack a room, don't start with the cupboards. Tidy up the clutter around the room before emptying the cupboards. If you empty the cupboards into an already untidy room, it will look so cluttered you'll probably give up.

Toilet cleaner

For a really spotless bowl (and a strain-free back) drop two Alka-Seltzer tablets into the water, wait twenty minutes, brush and flush!

Tight lids – 1

Some people turn jars upside down and bang the lid on a wooden surface: others get a cloth or put on rubber gloves and then twist them off. There are those who stretch an elastic band round lid and unscrew it that way, but the best way to loosen a stiff jar lid is it to immerse the lid in hot water or run it under a hot tap for a few minutes, then simply unscrew the lid.

Tight lids – 2

If you have a favourite jar, but find that the lid constantly sticks, try smearing a very thin layer of petroleum jelly around the thread. Your days of struggling against the odds to unscrew the lid will soon be a thing of the past.

Toothpaste

Take the unused key from a tin of sardines (you can always use a can opener to get at the fish later) and insert the flat end of your toothpaste tube in it. As you work your way down the tube, keep turning the key and you'll be surprised at how much longer the tube will last.

Tulips

To keep tulips fresh and upright for longer, wrap them in newspaper up to their necks and stand them in water for several hours before putting them in a vase.

Vacuuming

If your cleaner attachment is not long enough to get to a particularly out-of-the-way place, try using an empty wrapping paper tube as a temporary extension: you can even squeeze out the end of the tube to get into especially tight crevices.

Vase cleaner

If you have a stubborn stain on the bottom of a glass vase or cruet, fill it with water, drop in two Alka-Seltzers and when they've stopped fizzing, give the vase a shake and pour out the water.

Vinyl floor tiles

If one or two vinyl floor tiles need replacing, warm them with an iron. This softens the adhesive underneath and makes it easier to prise them off. Scrape the old adhesive from the floor and once you are sure that the replacement tiles are the exact size you need, warm them with an iron, spread fresh adhesive on the floor, put the new tile in place and weigh it down with bricks or a suitably heavy object until the adhesive is dry.

Wardrobe sense – 1

If you hang all your short garments at one end of the wardrobe, the chances are that there will be enough space under them for you to fit a double-height shoe rack or even a small chest of drawers.

Wardrobe sense – 2

When you take a garment off its hanger, always put that hanger at the end of the row. When you come to rehang it, you will know exactly where the hanger is and will avoid the tangle of hangers that is most people's wardrobes.

Washing-up liquid

Don't discard a seemingly empty bottle of washing-up liquid. Take the top off and half fill the bottle with water, or leave it standing overnight, cut the bottom off and add some water. Either way, you will have enough for about six more washes.

When it looks like snow

If snow is forecast take a shovel and keep it inside. That way, if the snow does fall and you have to clear the path, you won't have to tread through thick snow to get to where you usually keep your shovels.

Window cleaners

There's nothing more annoying than standing back to admire your freshly cleaned windows, seeing a huge streak and trying to work out if it's on the inside or out. If you use vertical strokes for one side and horizontal for the other, you may still get streaks, but at least you'll know which side they're on.

Windowsills

If you live in a town or city and you worry about your windowsills being grimy, tile them. Not only will they look good, they will be a lot easier to keep clean.

Winter wash

Do your windows ever run with condensation in winter and the condensation freezes over if there's a frost? You may not be able to stop the condensation forming but you can stop the frosting over by adding half a cup of antifreeze to each litre of water when you wash the windows.

Wills

If you own or part-own your home and you haven't made a will, make it now. Your spouse may automatically inherit, but if you die intestate, it takes much longer to get your affairs in order than it does if you leave a simple will. As long as your intentions are quite specific and the document is properly dated, signed and witnessed it's legal. But remember witnesses can't inherit.

Practical
Household Hints

Cleaning and
stain removal

OUT! OUT! DAMNED SPOT!

Before dishing the dirt on how to get rid of a nightmarish cocktail of stains, a few words of general advice. First, speed is of the essence. The quicker you act the better the chance that the stain won't leave a permanent mark.

- Non-greasy stains on washable fabric should be plunged into cold water as quickly as possible before taking specific action. And for carpets, a quick squirt from a soda syphon is the right action.

- Greasy stains should be sprinkled with talcum powder to absorb as much grease as possible. Brush it off after a few minutes and wash the garment as soon as you can.

- Highly coloured stains such as red wine or beetroot juice should be smothered in salt, which absorbs the moisture, and with it some of the colour. Leave for half an hour then vacuum up. Don't put salt on a carpet – it tends to stay in the pile and attract moisture, which can create permanent damp patches. Use kitchen paper instead.

- And never despair. You can always use dry cleaners and professional carpet cleaners.

And finally, always ensure that the colour won't run before applying stain remover of any kind. Find a patch of material that won't show should it not pass the test. Apply some of the stain remover to it and lay it between two pieces of white cloth. Press gently with a warm (not hot) iron. If the cloth stays white, fine. If the stain marks the cloth, don't be tempted to tackle it yourself – take the garment to the dry cleaners.

Acrylic paint

Blot the paint immediately and wash it out as quickly as you can with soap and cold water. If the paint has almost dried, scrape off as much as you can and do your best with proprietary dry-cleaning fluid, methylated spirit or paint removing solvent.

Antiperspirant stains

The best way of getting rid of antiperspirant stains is to treat them first with dry-cleaning solution and then with ordinary household

ammonia before rinsing the garment thoroughly. Alternatively,
apply a paste of bicarbonate of soda and salt to the area and leave
it for fifteen minutes before soaking in a biological detergent and
washing in the usual way.

Ballpoint pen stains

If the stained item is washable, soak the spot first in methylated
spirits and then in biological detergent before rinsing thoroughly.
If the item is non-washable, rub methylated spirits into the stain
and get it to the dry cleaner as soon as you can.

Beer stains

Sponge washable items right away with clean water then treat the
stain with a solution of one part white vinegar to five parts water.
(Caveat 1: Don't do this on acetate fabrics.) Rinse well, soak in
biological detergent and rinse again. If the stain persists, use a
solution of one part 20 vol. hydrogen peroxide in six parts of water
then wash in the hottest temperature the fabric will take. (Caveat 2:
Test this on a piece of fabric first to make sure that the solution
doesn't take the colour from it.) To clean a beer spillage try a squirt
or two from a soda syphon then use a good carpet shampoo, with
5ml vinegar for every 500ml of water.

Beetroot

If you've dribbled beetroot onto non-woollen clothes, take them off
as soon as you can and soak in cold water for as long as possible.
Then rub liquid detergent into the mark. That should do the trick: if
it doesn't, soak the offending garment in biological detergent,
sprinkle borax onto the stain, pour over boiling water then wash in
the usual way. If you've stained a woollen sweater, get it to the dry-
cleaner as quickly as possible.

Bird droppings

Scrape the bird dropping off then sponge the area with salt water
and soak in warm biological detergent. For non-washable items,
scrape the dirt off and soak in a mixture of 30ml household
ammonia in one litre of water. Leave overnight if possible then dab
any remaining marks with white vinegar.

Blood stains

As soon as blood has stained a piece of clothing, wash it in a solution of salt and cold (never warm) water. If it is an old stain and the blood has hardened, brush off as much as you can then soak the garment in a solution of cold water and either biological detergent or hydrogen peroxide. Why not warm water? Because the slightest heat seals in the mark forever!

Cellulose paint stains

Reach for the cellulose thinner as quickly as possible then wash the stained fabric in the usual way. These stains can only be removed from some synthetic fabrics such as rayon by being professionally dry cleaned and even the most expensive cleaners won't guarantee success – so best wear really old clothes when painting.

Chewing gum

To remove chewing gum from clothes freeze, or cover the gum with ice, then crack and scrape off. Any traces that are left will come out in the wash if you soak the affected garment in white vinegar or rub the stain with egg white before you put it in the machine.

Chocolate stains

If you're quick, it's often possible to remove a stray flake of chocolate from a garment with a quick flick of the finger before it starts to melt and leaves a stain. If not, dab it from the back with a mixture of soapy water and ammonia, then wash the garment in biological detergent. If that doesn't do the trick, rub dry borax into the stain, leave for half an hour then rinse. If that still doesn't work, rub the stain with glycerine, leave it for ten minutes and, again, rinse.

Cod liver oil stains

Be quick, for cod liver oil stains are almost impossible to remove after a minute or so. Scoop up as much as you can, then treat the mark from behind with the strongest liquid detergent you can find, rinse then wash as normal.

Coffee stains

A god soak in hand hot water to which biological detergent has been added is usually enough for all but the most stubborn coffee stains. Persistent ones usually succumb to being soaked for as long as necessary in methylated spirits or a solution of one part 20 vol. hydrogen to six parts of water, but best check for colourfastness before doing this. As a last resort, you could try stretching the stained material over a bowl, holding it in place with an elastic band, then pouring boiling water over it, sprinkling borax on the spot and giving it the boiling water treatment again.

Cola stains

A rinse in cold water, before dabbing from behind with liquid detergent then rinsing gets rid of most cola stains. If that doesn't work, try soaking in a mixture of methylated spirits, white wine and water before rinsing and washing well.

Creosote stains

Sponge the mark with eucalyptus oil then wash, or clean, as soon as you can.

Curry stains

Hold the stained fabric under running lukewarm water until it runs clear then rub in a solution of fifty percent glycerine and fifty percent warm water and leave for a while before rinsing, soaking in biological detergent and washing. If the stain is persistent and the fabric suitable, soak it in one part 20 vol. hydrogen peroxide to six parts cold water, rinse and wash.

Egg stains

Soak the fabric in biological detergent, unless the stain has set in which case soak in cold water first before treating with detergent. If it's a fried egg stain treat the stain as you would for fat (see below).

Emulsion paint stains

After scraping off as much as you can, inundate with cold water right away, rinse, flood again, rinse again and keep it up until the paint has gone. Then wash in the usual way, treating any residual marks with a grease solvent, available at most hardware stores.

Enamel paint stains

Paint remover worked into the back and front of the stain with a clean cloth and then a good wash should get rid of enamel paint stains. Never immerse the stained area in cold water until you are certain that the stain has gone otherwise it will become permanent.

Fat stains

Scrape off as much of the fat as you can and treat the stain with a proprietary grease solvent before washing the garment at the highest temperature it will stand.

Felt-tip pen stains

A good splash of methylated spirit before rubbing soap into the stain and giving the fabric a good wash should get rid of these increasingly common stains.

Foundation cream stains

Greasy stains made by some foundation creams often respond to dry-cleaning fluid, but the best way is to rub liquid detergent into the stain then flushing it out with warm water.

Fruit stains

Plunge the fabric in cold water. When no more colour is seeping from the stain, stretch the material over a heat-resistant bowl or pudding basin (using an elastic band or a piece of string to keep it in place), and pour very hot water over the stain. The more force the better, so hold the kettle as far from the bowl as possible. If the stain shifts, wash the fabric at the highest temperature it will stand. If it still won't shift, soak in a solution of one part 20 vol. hydrogen peroxide to six parts water.

General stains on clothing

Most types of baby wipes are a super standby for removing a stain from your clothing. They are also great for removing ink from your skin.

Gloss paint stains

Unless you have stained an acetate fabric, turpentine, white spirit of brush cleaner followed by a careful sponge with cold water and a normal wash should be just what the doctor ordered. If you have dribbled gloss paint on to acetate fabric, carefully scrape off as much as you can and take the garment to the dry cleaners.

Glue stains

Getting rid of adhesive stains depends on the kind of glue that has made its mark.

- Clear adhesive stains can be removed with non-oily nail-varnish remover or acetone.

- Contact adhesives submit to cold water as long as you catch them before they dry. Otherwise a good douse with methylated spirits will get rid of them.

- Epoxy adhesives (the ones that come with a separate hardener) will only come off if you catch them before the glue sets, in which case methylated spirits does the trick. But if the adhesive has hardened, nothing, not even all the dry cleaning in the world, will get rid of these stains.

- Latex adhesives can usually be removed with a cloth soaked in water if still wet, or scraped off if dry. Any residual stains can be removed with paintbrush cleaner used sparingly and with extreme caution (but never on delicate fabrics).

Hair dye stains

If you don't act right away, it's too late! A good soak in cold water, a quick rub with liquid detergent, then white vinegar should get of all but the most stubborn ones.

Hair lacquer stains

If you find that hair lacquer leaves marks on your clothes, treat them with amyl acetate then flush them out with dry-cleaning solvent.

Ice cream stains

Scrape off any residue with a blunt-edged knife, soak in biological detergent then attack any residual marks with dry-cleaning fluid. Dried-on stains can usually be removed by using a solution of one tablespoon of borax to 500ml of water sponged over the affected area.

Ink stains

To get an ink stain out, spray ultra-hold hairspray on the stain, let it dry, then wash as normal. Don't be afraid of putting too much hairspray on the stain. If there's still a mark, try treating it with a mix of lemon juice, ammonia and water in equal proportions.

Iodine stains

A ten-minute soak in a solution of one tablespoon of hypo crystals in 330ml of water should get these dark brown stains out in a flash.

Jam stains

If a soak in biological detergent followed by a good wash doesn't shift jam stains (or marmalade and honey) try a solution of one tablespoon of borax in 500ml of water or one part 20vol. hydrogen peroxide to six parts water.

Ketchup stains

After scraping off any excess, rinse in cold water then sponge with warm water, liquid detergent and, if the fabric is colourfast, a soak in one part 20 vol. hydrogen peroxide to six part of water. If the stain is still there, you could try methylated spirit and a good rinse. All of these methods should work for pickles and chutney, too.

Lipstick stains

You can use dry-cleaning solvent or methylated spirits to get rid of these stains. Whichever, once you have rubbed it in, wash the garment in a solution of liquid detergent and ammonia. Rubbing on some glycerine or petroleum jelly works, too.

Make-up stains

Scrape off as much as you can with a knife, being careful not to spread the stain. Then pat it with talcum powder to draw in any grease before washing in detergent and warm water. If the stain is really bad, try soaking the stained fabric in a solution of one teaspoon of ammonia to 500ml of warm water. (See also Mascara)

Mascara stains

Rub with neat washing-up liquid then wash as usual. Any stubborn residuals should vanish after being treated with dry cleaning fluid.

Mildew stains

Unless they are long established, mildew should surrender to ordinary laundering if the stains are rubbed with washing soap before the fabric is washed. White cotton and linen can be soaked in a solution of one tablespoon of bleach and one teaspoon of distilled white vinegar in one litre of water.

Milk stains

A rinse in cold water, a soak in biological detergent and a wash in warm detergent should remove milk stains.

Mud stains

Allow the mud to dry before brushing it off, working the fabric with a rubbing motion between your hands and washing in the usual way.

Mustard stains

Sponging the offending stain with warm water then soaking it in liquid detergent before giving it a good wash should remove mustard stains.

Nail varnish stains

Never smear the stain with nail varnish remover: it will only make things worse. Rather, treat the stain with amyl acetate or acetone before flushing the affected area with white spirit and washing it.

Newsprint

Washing in the usual way after sponging the stain with methylated spirit is the best way of getting rid of newsprint.

Nicotine stains

Rub your hands with lemon juice, then scrub with a pumice stone. Moisturize your hands to combat any dryness.

Orange juice stains

As soon as the juice has made its mark, soak the stain immediately in cold water then put it in the wash along with the rest of the laundry. If that doesn't do the trick completely, soak natural fabric in a solution of one part 20 vol. hydrogen peroxide to ten parts of water, and synthetic fabrics in two tablespoons of borax dissolved in a litre of warm water.

Oil paint stains

Holding a pad of clean white cloth under the stain, flood it immediately with white spirit. If necessary, dab with a proprietary stain remover then wash as usual.

Paint stains

(See acrylic, cellulose, emulsion, enamel, gloss, oil and watercolour paints.)

Paraffin stains

Keep the stained fabric away from a naked flame, paraffin stains are highly inflammable. Get rid of them by scraping off any excess then pat with talcum powder, cornflower or Fuller's earth to absorb as much of the grease as possible. Then treat the stain with a dry-cleaning solvent and wash at the hottest temperature the fabric will stand.

Perfume stains

To get rid of perfume stains, rub them with ordinary, household ammonia then wash the garment in liquid detergent. If the stain has dried-on, a solution of equal parts glycerine and warm water rubbed in, followed by a good wash, should get rid of it.

Perspiration stains

Unless the stain is really persistent, a soak in any proprietary biological detergent should get rid of it. But if it a really heavy stain, treat it with neat ammonia and a thorough rinse.

Old perspiration stains usually vanish if they are rinsed after being sponged with a solution of one tablespoonful of white distilled vinegar to 250ml warm water.

Petroleum jelly stains

Wash in the hottest water the fabric will stand after scraping off as much of the offending material as possible. If the stain is still there, use dry-cleaning solvent.

Plasticine stains

If the fabric is natural, scrape off as much as possible then rub the stain with grease solvent. If that fails, try lighter fuel on a piece of clean cloth. Before trying either of these on man-made fibres, check on an unseen part of the garment (the inside of a pocket or a seam, for example). In both cases, once the stain has gone, wash in the hottest water the fabric will take.

Putty stains

Put the garment in a freezer bag and leave it in the freezer for an hour or two before picking off the putty. Next, treat the stain with dry cleaning fluid before giving the garment a thorough, hot wash.

Red wine stains

Use lots of salt on red wine stains. Alternatively, a good splash of white wine will do the trick.

Salad dressing stains

Blot the dirty area with kitchen paper, then spray it with an aerosol grease solvent. That done, wash the fabric in the hottest water the garment will stand.

Scorch marks

Rub the fabric under running cold water, then soak it in a solution of two teaspoons of borax to one litre of warm water and wash as usual. If the stain is on white cotton or linen, any residual stain can usually be removed with bleach.

Scratches

Rubbing a Brazil nut on a scratch can disguise some surface damage in wooden furniture.

Shoe polish stains

After scraping off the excess, use white spirit to get rid of the mark, or if the fabric is tough (eg. denim) paintbrush cleaner is very effective. If the stain is small, a well-aimed squirt with an aerosol grease solvent will work. In either case, wash the item with detergent and hot water to which a little ammonia has been added.

Sick stains

Absorb or scrape off as much of the vomit as you can, then squirt with a soda syphon and sponge off with a borax solution. Wash as normal and the stain should vanish.

Soot stains

An aerosol dry cleaner is the answer to the question of soot and smoke stains.

Spirit stains

White spirits such as gin and vodka don't usually leave a stain, but if they do, they usually vanish in the wash. Whisky, red rum, and other spirit stains usually disappear in the washing after being sprayed with an aerosol dry cleaner.

Stool stains

Scrape off or absorb as much of the faeces as you can, then soak the underwear in a borax solution before washing it with a biological detergent.

Tar stains

After scraping off as much as you can, and softening what's left with some glycerine, remove the stain with eucalyptus oil, working from the back of the fabric. Wash the fabric at the highest temperature it will take and remove any residual marks with paintbrush solvent if the fabric is strong enough to take it.

Tea stains

Soak the afflicted cloth in a solution of 500ml warm water to 15ml borax. After half an hour, drain the water and soak again in a biological detergent then wash as usual. An old, dried-in stain should be softened with equal amounts of glycerine and warm water before being soaked as above. Really tough tea stains can usually be treated with methylated spirit – and if all else fails, white cotton can always be bleached.

Tobacco stains

Methylated spirit should remove these stains, or if the fabric is acetate, benzine. If that doesn't work, try equal parts of 20 vol.

hydrogen peroxide and water. Whichever, rinse well afterwards.

Turmeric stains

Try loosening the stain by soaking it in warm water and a little ammonia, then rubbing it with white spirit and finally giving it a good, hot wash. If the stain is on white cotton or linen, try using a weak bleach solution.

Urine stains

Absorb the urine by covering the mark with lots of salt then rinse the garments in cold water. If there is still a mark, treat it with undiluted household ammonia, rinse and apply white vinegar before washing as normal with a biological detergent.

Watercolour paint stains

A thorough rinse in cold water should completely fade most watercolour stains. If it doesn't, a little neat ammonia will.

White wine stains

Sprinkle salt on the stain, then soak it in cold water.

Wax stains

To remove melted wax from clothing lay a brown paper bag over the garment before ironing with a warm iron. Keep moving the bag around and it will absorb the wax. Any residual stains can be flushed out with dry cleaning solvent.

THE CLEANING CHORE

Cleaning may never be fun, but with a little planning and by following the hints herewith, it's not as bad as it could be.

Baking soda

Some scouring powders are too harsh for cleaning bathroom and kitchen fixtures: try baking soda instead. Not only does it clean, it removes odours and takes stains off refrigerators, coffee pots and a host of other things. It can also be used to deodorize nappy buckets.

Blenders

To clean out a blender, half-fill it with hot water, add a few drops of detergent and switch it on for a minute (make sure you remember to put the top back on first!). Then rinse it with warm water.

Burned-on food

Don't try and scrape badly burned-on food off pots and pans. It's much better to soak them overnight in biological washing powder. The residue will float off when you wash them the next morning.

Bread bins

If your bread bin becomes mildewed, wipe it with a cloth soaked in vinegar and leave the bin empty with the lid open until the smell has gone completely.

Cast iron pots

Don't scrub them too hard after use. Cast iron pots need a thin coating of lard or oil to stop them from rusting. It's much better simply to wipe them with kitchen paper after and before each use.

Cleaning cloths

Old cotton clothes can be used as dusters and cleaning rags. Never rub a used duster or cloth on polished wood – it could have little bits in it that scratch the surface, so always use a clean one.

Cleaning grouting

If the grouting between your tiles is dirty, try cleaning it with a typewriter rubber. Or cut a lemon in half and wipe the cut side over the grouting.

Cobwebs

If you wipe a cobweb off a wall, it may be sticky and leave a stain. So always lift them off, using a vacuum cleaner or a broom with a cloth tied round the head.

Cookers – 1

If you wipe the cooker top every time you've finished cooking grease won't build up and become baked on.

Cookers – 2

Pipe cleaners are ideal for cleaning the holes in the burners on gas cookers.

Curtains – 1

If you have just washed your curtains and they are not hanging too well, slip a curtain rod through the bottom hem of each panel and leave it there for a day or two. They will then hang beautifully.

Curtains – 2

When you wash your curtains or have them dry-cleaned, wash the curtain rods as well and give then give them a coating of wax – you will be amazed at how smoothly the curtains run when you rehang them.

Curtains – 3

Before you send your curtains to be cleaned, mark the places where the hooks should be inserted to make sure that you get them to hang as well as they were when you get them back. A simple blob of coloured nail varnish on the reverse side is just the job.

Crystal

To make your crystal glasses sparkle like new, rinse them in a weak solution of white vinegar and warm water.

Decanters

The best way to clean a glass decanter is to fill it with finely chopped pieces of raw potato, add water and shake it well.

Dusters

Make your dusters last longer and work more efficiently by soaking new ones in a solution of one part glycerine and one part water and allowing them to dry thoroughly before the first use.

Dusting

To do a thorough job, start at the door and work your way round the room in one direction to avoid spreading dust around.

Dustpans

If you dampen your dustpan before you start sweeping up, the dust will stay where it should be – in the pan – and won't roll out.

Egg-stained cutlery

Don't pour away the water you've boiled eggs in. Use it to soak cutlery stained with the yolk.

Grill pans

If you line your grill pan with aluminium foil before you use it every time, you hardly ever have to wash it. Simply take the foil off after grilling and apart from the rack there's nothing to wash.

Grinders

Remove stubborn morsels of meat from a grinder by running some raw potato or bread through it before you wash it.

Melted plastic

If you leave a plastic bag near the cooker and it melts, turn the cooker off and when it has cooled, nail varnish remover will get rid of the mess.

Mop head

Sponge mop heads dry out and crack and break up if they are not used. They will last much longer if you wrap yours in a plastic bag before you put them away after use.

Non-stick pans

Boiling water with a little bleach and vinegar before rinsing and washing can normally clean really grubby non-stick pans. After doing this, you'll need to grease them with a little olive oil to keep them non-stick.

Ovens

If something has been spilt in a hot oven, cover the affected area with salt and when the oven is cool, the residue should simply lift off.

Plastic table and worktops

For a spotlessly clean and shining surface, rub a little toothpaste onto it, then buff with a soft cloth.

Radiators – 1

If your central heating radiators are the old fashioned kind and you find them difficult to clean, try hanging a damp towel between them and blow the dust onto it with a hairdryer.

Radiators – 2

Dirty radiators give of less heat than clean ones, so always keep yours clean.

Rubber gloves

If your gloves are difficult to get on, dust the inside with talcum powder. When you take them off, dry them over an empty milk bottle: if you leave them wet, the rubber perishes.

Rusty knives

It doesn't happen very often, but if your knife becomes rusty, get rid of the rust with a damp cork dipped in scouring powder.

Saucepans – 1

Line your saucepans with kitchen foil to prevent vegetables sticking to the bottom.

Saucepans – 2

Scraping burnt-on food from a saucepan is a waste of time: it won't come off and you may well scratch the pan. Instead, fill the pan immediately with soapy water and leave to soak overnight.

Saucepans – 3

Boiling water discolours aluminium saucepans, but if you forget, clean them with vinegar and hot water.

Scouring powder

If you cover half the holes on the top of your can of scouring powder with masking tape, you will find that it lasts twice as long.

Silver – 1

Silver tarnishes if it becomes damp when stored in a drawer. You can prevent this from happening by putting a few pieces of chalk in with the silver. The chalk absorbs any moisture.

Silver – 2

Never wrap silver plate in ordinary paper – it damages the plating. Always use special acid-free paper for the purpose.

Sock it to them

Discard the duster and put an old sock over each hand when next you do the dusting. Using both hands will cut the time by half.

Stainless steel

You'll be surprised at how well stainless steel comes up if you polish it with old newspaper. Never be tempted to use bleach to remove stains from stainless steel cutlery and sinks. If they don't come off with a hot solution of detergent, use a proprietary stainless steel cleaner.

Teapots – 1

Heavily stained china teapots will sparkle like new if you soak them overnight in water and washing powder.

Teapots – 2

If your silver teapot is looking grotty inside put some washing soda dissolved in water with a few milk bottle tops inside the pot. Leave it for a few minutes then rinse.

Teapots – 3

To clean a teapot spout, pack is as tightly as possible with salt and leave it overnight before flushing it out.

Teapots – 4

Clean the inside of a metal teapot by filling it with water, dissolving a tablet for cleaning false teeth in it and leave overnight.

Teapots – 5

An infrequently used silver teapot can give tea an unpleasant taste. You can prevent this by dropping a couple of sugar lumps into it and propping up the lid before despatching it to the back of the cupboard.

The tidy bag

To pick up paper clips and similar items when vacuuming, tape a small paper bag to the handle and drop these little annoyances into it as you go.

The tidy box

Keep a box under the stairs or in a convenient cupboard and put anything you find out of place in it. Once a month threaten to take the contents to a charity shop and you'll be surprised at how tidy the family becomes – especially if you actually do take everything to the local charity shop.

The tidy trolley

Keep all your cleaning things – polishes, glass cleaners, dusters, brush and pan etc in a trolley on wheels. When you are cleaning pull it round with you and everything you will need is instantly to hand.

The two-bucket trick

Next time you are mopping the floor, make the cleaning solution last longer by using the two-bucket technique. Put your cleaner in one bucket of water and have another bucket alongside to squeeze your mophead into before dipping it into the one with the grubby water. If you use your kitchen rubbish bucket as the one with the cleaner in it, you will end up with a spotless floor and a clean bucket, as well!

Tin openers

Feeding a piece of kitchen paper through the jaws of a tin opener will keep it clean.

Vacuum first

Always vacuum before dusting as hoovering raises clouds of dust. And if you have to vacuum woodwork or other surfaces that may scratch, attach a piece of foam around the head of the vacuum attachment and keep it there with a rubber band.

Vacuum flasks

Handy they may be, but if you use them over and over again and simply just rinse them under a tap, they can become badly stained on the inside. Clean them by filling them with hot water, adding some rice and giving them a good shake.

Venetian blinds

The easiest way of cleaning these notoriously difficult-to-clean blinds is to soak a pair of fabric gloves in soapy water, put them on and slide each slat, one by one, between your fingers. Easy!

Varnished woodwork

Next time you have to clean a varnished wooden surface, wipe cold black tea over the surface, then buff with a soft, dry cloth

Washing up – 1

Soak dishes with starchy food like potatoes or egg on them in cold water, not hot or warm: soak greasy ones in hot water with a little detergent squished into it.

Washing up – 2

Plunging delicate china and glass bottom first can crack them. It's much better to slide them sideways into the water.

Washing up – 3

Use a plastic bowl when washing precious china and glass – if they slip through your fingers there's less chance of them smashing.

Washing up – 4

Always wash non-greasy items first.

Washing up – 5

Don't wash china that is especially fragile – it's much better to clean it with Fuller's Earth.

Washing walls – 1

If you are thinking of having your walls repainted simply because they look grubby, have them professionally cleaned instead. The will come up like new at about a third of the cost of having them professionally repainted.

Washing walls – 2

If you wash walls starting at the bottom, when you move upwards, the cleaner solution will drip on to the part you've just washed. But if you start at the top, it may cause permanent drip stains as it drips down. To avoid this, start at the bottom, working quickly over a small area at a time, wiping the wall dry with a sponge or well-wrung-out cloth as you go. Problem solved!

Wooden surfaces – 1

The best way to keep wooden surfaces clean is to scrub them with scouring powder, then rub in a little olive oil afterwards to build up a seal.

Wooden surfaces – 2

Don't wax wooden kitchen tables and cabinets when you are polishing them. It traps grease, which will soften the surface. Use a waxless furniture polish.

Practical Household Hints

Cook's tour

We can't all be Delia Smith or Jamie Oliver. But do they and the other stars of the kitchen know that if you keep a couple of pieces of dried orange peel in the tea or teabag caddy, even the cheapest, supermarket own brand tea tastes as if it had been made for the gods? Or that the best way to cut a pizza into slices is to use kitchen scissors...

Artichokes – 1

Adding a few drops of lemon juice or vinegar in which artichokes are boiling brings out the flavour.

Artichokes – 2

If you stand artichokes in cold water to which a dash of vinegar has been added, they won't discolour.

Asparagus – 1

Limp, uncooked asparagus will perk up if you leave stand it upright in a jug containing just a little water, cover it with a plastic bag and put it in the fridge for half an hour. If, on the other hand the lower stalks look very tough, use a potato peeler to remove the outer layer.

Asparagus – 2

If you don't have a special asparagus cooker, there are two ways to cook this delicious vegetable. Stand a can with both top and bottom removed in a suitably sized saucepan of water (one that is slightly taller than the asparagus) and stand the asparagus in the can. The other way is put it in the container part of your coffee percolator – as long as all traces of coffee have been removed.

Baine Marie

When cooking something in a baine Marie, put a couple of pebbles or marbles in the bottom of the pan. The pebbles will rattle should the pan begin to boil dry.

Baked fruit and vegetables

Stuffed baked tomatoes, peppers and apples all keep their shape if you stand them in cake patty tins in the oven.

Beetroot

To keep cooked beetroot red cook them whole with about three centimetres of the stalk on them. Adding a little vinegar to the cooking water will help them keep their colour.

Boiling milk

If milk is threatening to boil over, take it off the heat and put it down on the work surface with a heavy bump (not heavy enough to make it spill over). The bump stops the milk going over the top.

Broccoli

If you want evenly cooked broccoli cut an X incision into the stems from the end towards the top.

Burned casseroles

Turn a burned casserole out into another container. The food that comes away from the casserole dish will be quite edible. Don't scrape the bottom of the pan, though – the bits that stick will taste awful.

Burned milk

If you do burn milk, you can get rid of the taste by adding a pinch of salt to the saucepan.

Cake decoration

The cheat's way to get a professional pattern on the top of a cake is to put a paper doily on top of the cake and sift caster sugar over it. Carefully remove the doily and that's all there is to it.

Cakes

If a cake you are baking sinks in the middle, cut out the soggy centre bit, fill it with cream and fruit and serve it as dessert rather than cake.

Canapés – 1

In an emergency, when you offer someone a drink and you're out of nibbles, cut some slices of bread in to 2.5cm squares, drizzle olive oil and some dried herbs on them and pop them in a hot oven for a minute or two, until they start to crisp.

Canapés – 2

Cut bacon rashers into 2.5cm strips and crisp them up in the oven. They make tasty cocktail snacks.

Carving meat

When carving a joint of meat, put the carving board on a damp towel. It stops the board slipping all over your work surface.

Cauliflower

To keep cauliflower a lovely, natural creamy white, add just a touch of milk to the cooking water.

Cheese

When storing cheese you can keep it fresh for longer by wrapping it in a vinegar soaked cloth and keeping it in a sealed container.

Chips

Shaking freshly fried chips in a clean paper bag gets rid of any excess grease.

Chocolate

The best way to melt chocolate is to make an aluminium foil cup, butter it slightly and put the squares of chocolate in that. Pop it in a warm oven for a few minutes and then the chocolate will melt beautifully. Not only that, it will slide out without sticking.

Cloudy stock

If home made stock comes out cloudy, return it to the heat, add two or three pieces of eggshell and let it simmer for a few minutes. This will clear it. Eggshells also clear cloudy consommé. Remember to take the shell out before using the stock or serving the soup!

Coffee

If you wish to reuse coffee grounds spread them on a baking tray and cook them for thirty minutes at 180°C/350°F, Gas mark 4. Mix them fifty/fifty with freshly ground beans when next you feel the need of a caffeine blast.

Cooking with butter

If you are frying things in butter, add a little oil to the frying pan. The butter is much less likely to brown.

Corn

Line the bottom of the pot you're cooking corn on the cob in with the green leaves that you usually throw away. The corn retains more flavour this way.

Cream

Make whipped cream go further by folding in some stiffly whisked egg white just before you serve it.

Crumbs!

To make breadcrumbs roughly crumble bread slices and put them in a hot oven. When they are crisp, put them in a paper bag and reduce them to crumbs with a rolling pin.

Curdled hollandaise

If your hollandaise sauce starts to curdle, pour it into a cold bowl and give it a gentle whisk before returning it to the pan and reheating it gently.

Custard

Stop a skin forming on a custard by sprinkling icing sugar on the surface and then stirring it in before serving.

Dough

Experienced bread makers rest their kneaded dough in a greased plastic bag. The dough rises faster, doesn't form a crust and it won't stick to the plastic.

Dried herbs

If you are using dried herbs in a recipe that lists fresh herbs in the ingredients, always use half the amount. The dried variety has a much more intense flavour.

Dumplings

Steam herb dumplings for soups and stews in an egg poacher.

Eggs – 1

Eggs won't crack, even if you take them straight from the fridge, if you put them into lukewarm water first and then bring them to the boil.

Eggs – 2

If you fancy a boiled egg and the only ones in the fridge are cracked, wrap them in aluminium foil and boil them as normal. And if you rub a little salt in the crack first, it will save you the trouble of salting the egg when it's cooked.

Eggs – 3

If an egg starts to crack in the boil, you can stop the white escaping by adding some salt or vinegar to the water. It seals the white and keeps it where it should be – inside the egg.

Eggs – 4

To prevent hard-boiled eggs acquiring a black ring around the yolk, plunge them into cold water immediately after you've boiled them.

Eggs – 5

Stop boiled eggs from cracking in the water by very carefully piercing the egg with a pin before putting it in the water.

Energy saver

If you wrap two lots of different vegetables in aluminium foil, you can boil them in the same pot without the taste of one affecting the flavour of the other.

Fatty stews

Blotting the top of an overfatty stew with kitchen paper will remove most of the surplus fat. But if there is still some grease, one or two ice cubes dropped into the pot will remove it as the fat congeals around them and can easily be lifted out.

Fluffy meringues

When making meringues, add a teaspoon of cornflour to every 112 grams of sugar. It stops them going toffeeish and sticky.

Freezing vegetables

Before you freeze vegetables you should blanch them. The best way to do this if you have a deep fat fryer is to make sure it's spotlessly clean, fill it half-way with water and bring it to the boil, put the vegetables in a chip basket and plunge them into the bubbling water for about 30 seconds. If you don't have a fryer, use a saucepan and a metal salad shaker.

French beans

You can cook French beans straight from the freezer by putting them in a hot frying pan with some just-cooked strips of bacon. If you have some fresh French beans that have started to wilt, put them in a polythene bag and chill them in the fridge. This will make them crisper.

Fried onions

Avoid burning chopped onions by covering them with water and adding a knob of butter. Boil them until the water has evaporated, then lower the heat and continue cooking until they are golden. And to brown them more quickly, add a little sugar to the pan when the water has boiled away.

Fruit cakes

When you're mixing the ingredients for a fruit cake, sift in a quarter of a teaspoon of mustard for every 225 grams of flour. The mustard enhances the fruit flavour and gives the cake a lovely rich colour. And if you want to give the cake a nutty flavour, stir in a tablespoonful of crunchy peanut butter. (If you do this always tell anyone you offer a slice to that the cake has nuts in it. Nut allergy can cause a violent, sometimes fatal, reaction in some people.)

Frying

Don't fry food in olive oil alone – it doesn't get hot enough. Use half olive oil and half sunflower, rape or corn oil.

Gammon and bacon

The best way to de-salt these is to put them in a pan of cold water, bring to the boil, and then throw the water away. That done, repeat the process before cooking in the usual way.

Garlic

Hit garlic cloves with the side of a heavy knife (or a meat tenderizer) and the skin will slide off a treat.

Garlic salt

To make your own garlic salt sprinkle lots of salt onto a board and crush a clove of garlic over it. Store in an airtight jar.

Glowing glazes

When you glaze homemade pastry with an egg yolk to give it a golden glow, add a pinch of salt to the egg first.

Goose

Before cooking your goose, stick an apple inside it to mop up the excess fat. Do this with duck as well.

Hamburgers

Burgers cook quicker if you poke a hole through the middle with a skewer before putting them on the barbie or under the grill. By the time they have cooked through, the hole will have sealed.

Hot curries

If you planned a mild chicken tikka and you've ended up with a vindaloo, cool it down by stirring in some natural yoghurt.

Hot oil test

If you want to be sure that your cooking oil is at the right temperature, drop a small cube of bread into it when it's heated. If the bread cooks to a golden brown in a minute, the oil is ready for use.

Hot pancakes

Stack cooked pancakes on a plate and put it over a saucepan of boiling water and cover them with a tea towel. They'll stay warm all through teatime!

Icing

Always dip the knife you are using to ice a cake in a cup of boiling water to heat the blade. This stops the icing clinging to the knife and it will spread evenly on the cake.

Jam

To stop a scum forming on home-made jam, add a knob of butter to it when it's boiling.

Jellies – 1

If you're making a jelly well in advance of when it's going to be used, stop a skin forming on it by running a knob of butter over it when it's still hot. This also stops skins forming on puddings and sauces.

Jellies – 2

To help jelly to set quickly melt half the jelly in half the amount of boiling water specified and make up the balance with ice cubes.

Kippers – 1

Kippers won't dry out in the grill pan if you put a little water in it before sliding it under the heat.

Kippers – 2

Skewer kippers through the tail and hang them in a pot of boiling water. Not only are they healthier to eat this way, there's no messy pan to clean afterwards. You can freeze the kipper water and use it as fish stock.

Lumpy sauces – 1

To achieve a smooth, lump-free sauce, combine all the ingredients in the blender first than bring to the boil, stirring carefully with a balloon whisk.

Lumpy sauces – 2

If your sauce is lumpy and you don't have time to remake it ,pour the sauce into a screw-top jar, shake very vigorously and the lumps will disappear.

Melba toast

The easiest way to make Melba toast is to cut some sliced bread into very small squares, roll them until they are thin with a rolling pin, and bake them in a low oven until they start to brown.

Meringue tops

To stop meringue tops from weeping when they come into contact with the contents of a lemon (or any) meringue pie, beat the egg whites over a pan of hot water.

Minced meat sauces

Stretch these by adding two tablespoonfuls of porridge oats to every 450 grams of mince.

Mocha

If you fancy a cup of Mocha and don't have the proper ingredients in the store cupboard, make a cup of hot chocolate and stir in a teaspoon of instant coffee.

Mushrooms

The best way to slice mushrooms is to use an egg slicer.

Off the boil

A matchstick placed between the lid and the upright sides of a saucepan, lets out some of the steam and stops the water from boiling over without affecting the cooking time.

Omelettes

For a really fluffy omelette add a splash of soda water to the egg. This also makes scrambled eggs light and fluffy.

Onions

If you are serving boiled onions and want to keep them from disintegrating in the simmering water, cut a cross in the stem end.

Oversalted soup

If you have oversalted the soup, try adding a little sugar to it.

Oversalted stew

Add a few pieces of raw, peeled potato to an oversalted stew and if it doesn't absorb all the excess salt it will at least absorb enough to make the dish edible.

Pastry – 1

Never use all the pastry if you are baking blind. Always keep a little bit and cut it into strips to repair any cracks that appear.

Pastry – 2

Never roll freshly made pastry right away. Cover it and put it in the refrigerator for about fifteen minutes. And when rolling it, never stretch it by hand: it will only shrink back to size again when its in the oven.

Pasta – 1

To reheat cooked pasta, drop it in boiling water for 30 seconds and it's almost as good as fresh.

Pasta – 2

Don't break up spaghetti to get it into the saucepan. Once the water has boiled, gently push one end into the pan. As it softens, coil it round until all the pasta is in the water and cooking.

Pasta – 3

If you put a chip basket or a large strainer in the pasta pan before filling it with water, the cooked pasta is easier to lift out when it's ready.

Pasta – 4

Stop your pasta sticking together by rinsing it well under a running tap before cooking it. If you forget and it does glue together, it may loosen if you let the water cool and bring it back to the boil again.

Pasta – 5

The spaghetti pan won't boil over if you add a knob of butter to the water. A teaspoonful of olive oil also works.

Peas in the pod

Don't shell peas before you cook them, try cooking them in the pod instead. When they are ready, the pods open and float to the top. The peas are easy to remove and taste better.

Pies

Rather than the usual porcelain funnel to keep the pastry up and let the steam out in a savoury pie, why not use a ring of chopped marrow bone? It does the job just as well and adds an extra flavour to the pie.

Poached eggs

To set the white of a poached egg and keep it in good shape, add a tablespoonful of vinegar to the water.

Popcorn

Empty cooked popcorn into a deep-fry basket. Give it a shake and the unpopped bits will slip through.

Pork chops

Soak pork chops in boiling water for about three minutes before you cook them. Then blot them dry before they are consigned to the frying pan or grill tray. They will taste much better.

Potato salad

Add olive oil and vinegar to hot potatoes for a delicious potato salad that can be served either hot or cold.

Potatoes – 1

For perfect, crisp roast potatoes, forget about dredging them with flour halfway through the roasting time. Instead, parboil them, drain off the water and shake them around so that the surface starts to break just a little. Now roast them. And if you can use goose fat, potatoes cooked in it are extra special.

Potatoes – 2

If you overcook your potatoes and they turn to soup, don't despair. Add a little dried milk or instant potato powder, a knob of bitter and beat them into a delicious puree.

Potatoes – 3

The best way to reheat beaked potatoes is to dip them in hot water first before consigning them to the oven.

Pre-cooked poached eggs

As soon as an egg is poached, put it in a bowl of cool water until you are ready to eat, at which point reheat it for a minute in hot water.

Pulses

A sprinkling of baking powder added to the cooking water stops haricot beans and other large pulses cracking and disintegrating while cooking. Don't salt the water, pulses should be salted after they have been cooked, not before or during otherwise they go hard.

Quick potted cheese

Grate the ends of slabs of cheese, mix with butter, beat in a little dry sherry and pour into suitable sized containers. Cover with melted butter and keep in the fridge for an emergency starter.

Red cabbage

Red cabbage stays red and won't go purple if you add a drop or two of vinegar to the water while it's cooking.

Reheated stews

Unless they have been frozen, always reheat stews and casseroles by bringing them slowly to the boil and cooking at that heat for ten minutes to ensure that no bacteria remain.

Rhubarb! Rhubarb!

You can make you rhubarb a bit less acid if you cook it in black tea instead of water.

Rice – 1

A failsafe method for perfectly cooked, fluffy rice every time is to cover the rice with salted water to a thumb's length above the rice. Bring the water to the boil and let it bubble for a minute, then turn off the heat. By the time all the water has been absorbed, the rice is just right, and still piping hot.

Rice – 2

Rice stays white if you add some lemon juice to the water.

Rice – 3

The easiest way to make rice pudding is to put rice and sugar in a wide-necked vacuum flask, add boiling milk and leave it for twelve hours.

Rice – 4

If you burn rice, tip it into a fresh saucepan, cover it with as many slices of bread as necessary, put the lid on and leave it for a minute or two. The bread will absorb the burned taste.

Saffron substitute

Made from the dried pistils of the crocus, saffron is expensive. Old English or pot marigold petals may not have the same flavour, but they enrich the colour of the dish.

Sandwiches

If you are making sandwiches for a large group, cream the butter and filling together in the blender. It's easier to spread and tastes exactly the same!

Sausages – 1

To brown sausages evenly roll them in flour before frying them.

Sausages – 2

Before grilling sausages, skewer them together in pairs. Much easier to turn that way!

Scrambled eggs

Take scrambled eggs off the heat when they are three-quarters cooked. They will finish cooking on their own and the pan will be easier to clean afterwards.

Self-stirring sauces

After a sauce (or stew) has started to thicken, drop a large, clean marble into the saucepan. The heat moves it around the bottom and saves you the effort of stirring the sauce.

Shepherd's pie

To prevent meat sticking to the bottom of the pie dish, line it with a few rashers of bacon. This also works with meat loaf. Not only will it be easier to clean the dish, the bacon lends its flavour to the meat as well.

Sherry

A dash of sherry added to tinned soup lifts a dull dish onto a higher level altogether.

Soggy cornflakes

If you breakfast cereal has gone soggy, sprinkle them on a baking tray and put them in a warm oven for ten minutes or so. They'll crisp up good as new.

Soup

Drizzle some finely grated raw carrot into soups just before serving. It gives the soup a lovely rich colour and lends it extra flavour.

Sour cream

Make your own sour cream by adding a tablespoon of lemon juice to each 300ml of fresh cream.

Spaghetti Bolognaise

To eke out spaghetti bolognaise, soak some day-old bread in milk, squeeze it out and whiz it in the blender before adding it to the meat sauce.

Spices

If you make your own chutneys and pickles and also have an individual tea infuser, put chopped cinnamon and cloves in it and use it in the making. When the preserve is ready all you have to do is take out the infuser and there are no annoying pieces of uncooked spices in the finished product.

Sponges

The best way to remove a sponge from the cake tin is to put the tin – sponge intact – on a damp cloth and leave it there for two or three minutes. The heat of the sponge makes the cloth steam very gently and this makes it much easier to turn the sponge out.

Stale bread

Revive stale bread by wrapping it in foil and putting it in a hot oven – 230°C/450°F, Gas mark 8 – for ten minutes. Remember to let the foil cool before unwrapping it.

Stale buns

You can freshen up stale buns by dipping them in milk and heating them in a cool oven. And if you smear them with butter no one would ever guess that they were about to be thrown out.

Stock cubes

If you are using a bouillon stock cube, put a little mince in the water. It gives the stock a much richer, more home-made flavour.

Stuffing

If you have made too much stuffing for the fowl, wrap the excess in sausage-shaped aluminium foil parcels and cook them in the roasting pan.

Tender beef

If you are making a beef casserole, add a teaspoonful of vinegar to the recipe. It makes the meat more tender and brings out the flavour in the gravy.

Thickener

Instant potato makes an excellent thickener for soups and stews as do pureed potatoes.

Tomatoes

Adding just a pinch of sugar to tomatoes while they are cooking brings out their flavour superbly.

Too much garlic

If you have been over-generous with the garlic in a stew or casserole, add a handful of chopped parsley to make it more palatable.

Vegetables

When defrosting blocks of frozen vegetables, pour boiling water over them before cooking. Not only does this rinse away the frost, the vegetables retain their flavour better, too.

White meringues

For meringues that are whiter than white, slip a wooden board under the baking tray. It absorbs any smoke, which discolours the meringues.

White mushrooms

If you like to keep your mushrooms white, add a teaspoonful of lemon juice to the butter when frying them. And if you shake the pan frequently (and carefully) they will sauté and stay firm, rather than steam and go soggy.

Yorkshire pudding

To make a really light Yorkshire pudding (or pancakes), separate the egg, beat in the yolk then whip up the egg white and fold it into the mixture last of all.

KEEPING YOUR COOL

Some tips on freezing and refrigeration.

Beans and pulses

Soak pulses, dried beans and peas then freeze them. They can be used straight from the freezer in casseroles and stews – especially handy if you need to make a meal stretch that little bit further.

Cake leftovers

Don't throw these away. If you keep them in the freezer, it won't be long before you have a permanent source of trifle base to hand.

Cake mixes

Thoughtful home-bakers fill patty tins with cake-mix, freeze it and then decant it into plastic bags. If ever they have unexpected visitors, all they have to do is defrost it in the microwave and pop it in the oven. By the time the kettle's boiled, the house is filled with the delicious smell of home baking.

Cakes and sponges

Slice these and wrap the individual slices in greaseproof paper before freezing. That way you will only need to defrost as much as you need, rather than the whole lot.

Chives and parsley

If you freeze unchopped chives and parsley, you won't have to stretch for the chopping board when you come to use them. They'll be so brittle, all you have to do is grate or crumble over whatever you're seasoning.

Chops and cutlets

Freeze chops, cutlets (and fish) between sheets of greaseproof paper. You'll find that they're easier to separate when you come to defrost them.

Cottage cheese

The slimmer's friend stays fresher longer if it is stored upside down in the refrigerator.

Ice cream

Cut large blocks of ice cream into individual portions. That way you only need take out as much as you need.

Ice cubes

If you store ice cubes in polythene bags, spray them with soda water before you put them in the freezer. It stops them sticking together.

False cream

A good sustitute for real cream is evaporated milk. Boil an unopened tin in water for twenty minutes. It whips up to double its size and does a fair imitation of the real thing.

Fruit

If you line the salad drawer with kitchen paper before you put your fruit in it, any excess moisture is drawn into the paper and the fruit stays fresher longer.

List it

Keep a list of contents on the inside door of your fridge or freezer and you will know at a glance what you have in stock.

Milk

If you have bought too much milk and there isn't enough room for it all in the fridge, stand the bottles or cartons in a bowl of cold water with a few ice cubes floating in it. Cover the containers with a clean tea towel with the ends dipping in the water.

Pancakes

Don't be caught short on Shrove Tuesday. Make your pancakes the weekend before and freeze them between sheets of greaseproof paper. Defrost them on a griddle, under the grill at low heat, or in the toaster at the lowest setting. If they don't defrost first time, put them in at the same setting again.

Power cuts

If your area suffers a power cut, keep the freezer door firmly shut and open the kitchen windows to keep the room well ventilated. Food in a well-stocked freezer should stay frozen for at least eight hours. If things start to defrost, don't take any risks, throw everything out and check your insurance policy.

Sandwiches

Find time on a Sunday to make sandwiches for a week's worth of packed lunches. Freeze them in packets, one packet for each day, take them out the night before and they'll defrost by breakfast.

Stop slippage

Small items often slip through the bottom of a freezer basket. To stop this annoying tendency, line the bottom of the basket with some netting. Not only does it keep food in its place, it encourages the air to circulate.

Spacesavers

If you are making soups to freeze, use half the liquid the recipe calls for. Add the rest when you defrost it.

STORING FOOD

Artichokes

Artichokes will last for at least a week in the fridge if you wrap them unwashed in a piece of damp towelling and store them in a plastic bag.

Avocados

Accelerate the softening of hard avocados by putting them in bowl along with a ripe banana.

Bananas

Don't store bananas in the fridge, they'll go black. And don't store ripe bananas in the fruit bowl along with other fruit – they'll over-ripen it.

Bacon

Don't keep packets of bacon flat in the fridge. If you roll them up and store them that way, the rashers won't stick together.

Bacon rinds

If you keep the bits you usually throw away and put them, diced, into stews and casseroles, they give them added flavour.

Biscuits

If you put two sugar lumps in the biscuit tin, they absorb moisture and keep your biscuits nice and crisp.

Bread

To keep bread fresher for longer, put a stick of celery in the bread bin. Renew it once a week (or as soon as it starts to go brown and limp) and you need never have stale bread again.

Carrots

To keep carrots moist cut the top off before you store them.

Cheese – 1

Don't keep cheese in its plastic wrapping. As soon as you can, take it from the pack and wrap it in foil. This stops it getting sweaty.

Cheese – 2

If you are not storing your cheese in a refrigerator, to stop it going mouldy put a sugar lump on it before wrapping it in foil. The sugar absorbs the moisture that makes the cheese go off.

Crumbs

Keep leftover crumbs from the bottom of cereal packets in an airtight jar and scatter them over stews (or fruit crumbles) for a tasty,
crunchy topping.

Eggs – 1

Eggs will stay fresh for up to a month if you smear the shells with a thick coating of glycerine as soon as you get them home and store them small end upward.

Eggs – 2

If you're using a recipe that calls for eggs whites, put the yolks in a suitable container, cover them with water and they'll stay fresh for several days.

Eggs – 3

If, on the other hand, your recipe calls for yolks and not whites, store the white in an airtight container and they should stay fresh in the fridge for about a week.

Eggs – 4

Never store onions and eggs alongside each other. Eggshells are porous and absorb the onion's flavour.

Fruit cake

If you have a moist fruitcake to store, put a slice of apple in the cake tin. It will keep the cake good and moist.

Grated rind

Don't throw any leftover orange and lemon rind away. Put it in a screw-top jar along with some caster sugar and use it flavour cakes and puddings.

Green tomatoes

Tomatoes that are too green to eat can be ripened (and will keep their moisture) if they are wrapped in newspaper and stored in a cool, dark cupboard or drawer.

Jam – 1

Keep the waxed paper from cereal packets and cut it into circles to seal jars when making jam.

Jam – 2

If you allow home-made jam to cool and thicken a little before you put it into jars, the fruit won't sink to the bottom.

Lemon juice

Pierce one end of the lemon with a cocktail stick or toothpick, squeeze out as much juice as you need and plug the hole with the stick. The lemon will last much longer and keep fresh until you've squeezed it dry.

Lemons

Whole lemons will stay fresh for weeks if you put them in a plastic box in the refrigerator.

Lettuce

When storing washed lettuce in the fridge, don't seal the plastic bag it's in: keep it loose and open and it will last for a week. This works for parsley and watercress, too.

Oil – 1

If you must reuse cooking oil, always strain it immediately after using it and store it out of direct light.

Oil – 2

If olive oil is out of your price range, put a few olives at the bottom of your bottle of salad-dressing oil. They will flavour the oil, although it won't be quite as good as the real thing.

Olive oil

Lengthen the life of your olive oil by adding just a pinch of sugar to it and keeping it in the fridge.

Onions

To keep half an onion fresh, rub the cut side with butter.

Pears

To ripen hard pears, put them in a paper bag with a ripe apple.

Peaches

To ripen peaches lay them in a box and cover them with several layers of newspaper.

Pepper

If you prefer to use pre-ground pepper, add a few peppercorns to the pepper pot. They prevent the holes from clogging up and enliven the taste of the pepper.

Peppers

A scooped out red, green or yellow pepper makes an unusual and stylish holder for mayonnaise.

Salad dressing

Whatever the recipe, mix your salad dressing in an old, clean screw-top coffee jar. You can keep what you don't use in the fridge and add to it as necessary.

Salads

Never use metal salad servers. Metal bruises lettuce leaves and turns the edges brown, so always use wooden ones.

Salt

To stop salt clogging up with lumps, add a few grains of rice to the salt shaker. By absorbing any moisture, they keep the salt bone dry and running smoothly.

Sauces

If you have made too much sauce and don't want to throw the excess away, cover the surface with greaseproof paper before putting the sauceboat in the fridge. This will stop a skin forming.

Stock

Don't throw away the bones from the Sunday joint of poultry. They make the basis of a great stock if you boil them in a pressure cooker – it also freezes a treat. If you don't have the time to make the stock immediately, wrap the bones, put them in the freezer and make the stock at your leisure.

Strawberries

Don't keep strawberries in a bowl in the fridge: rather put them in a sieve, put the sieve in the bowl and then put the bowl in the fridge. This allows air to circulate around them and keeps them fresh.

Sweet pie crusts

Add sweetness to your fruit pies by painting egg white around the edge of the pastry and sprinkling it with caster sugar.

Sweets

To stop sweets sticking together, sprinkle them with castor sugar.

Tomato puree...

... and other concentrates that are leftover can be frozen in an ice-cube tray and kept in the freezer for future use.

Vanilla sugar

Vanilla sugar adds a lot of *je ne sais quois* to lots of recipes for sweets and baking – but it can be expensive to buy. It's easy to make your own simply by putting a vanilla pod in a jar of caster sugar and storing it in a cool place out of the light.

Vegetable water

Don't throw the water away after boiling vegetables. Freeze it and add it to stock and sauces for extra flavour.

Practical Household Hints

DIY

A wise old sage on hearing the expression 'A job worth doing, is worth doing well' said, 'If a job is worth doing, it's worth paying someone else to do it properly.' DIY enthusiasts would disagree.

Accurate measuring

When you are measuring things, always have the tape or rule straight on with your eyes right in front or directly above the point at which you are taking the reading. Anywhere else and there's a fair chance that your reading won't be accurate.

Battery terminals

Coat a little petroleum jelly on the terminals of your car battery. It will prevent corrosion.

Broken china

Next time you are gluing broken china, smear some petroleum jelly round the edges of the break. It stops any surplus glue that oozes out from setting. When you have finished, simply wipe the jelly off with a damp cloth.

Candle trick

If you have painted a door and allowed it to dry, rub the edges with a candle before you close it. This stops the door sticking.

Car washing

Own-brand, supermarket dishwashing detergent cuts through the dirt as well as the much more expensive washes for sale at garages. And when washing your car, start with the roof, washing and rinsing in small sections so that the soap doesn't have a chance to dry and leave streak marks. An old bath towel is ideal for drying, before polishing with the best chamois you can afford.

Colour co-ordinating – indoors

If you like your painted wall to match or tone with the curtains, carpets and upholstery, dab some of the paint you intend to use for the walls on to a piece of white paper. That way you will an instant colour guide when you go shopping. Always remember to colour match in the daylight – the lights in showrooms can be deceptive.

Colour co-ordinating – outdoors

If you paint any outbuildings – shed, garage and the like – the same colour scheme as you used for your house, you will give your property an attractive, unified appearance.

Concealing a nailhead

If you want to hide your nailheads, chisel a small shaving parallel to the grain of the wood, at the point where the nail is to be hammered in, leaving the end of the shaving attached to the surface. Once the nail is in, fix the shaving back in place with a suitable adhesive.

Cracks

If you see a crack in an outside wall and you are not sure if it indicates a structural problem bridge over the surface with a layer of plaster of Paris. If it cracks within two months, call in a builder for you could have subsidence.

Decanting paint

If you have bought a large tin of paint, decant some of it into a smaller can to use as you work. Smaller cans are much easier to handle than large ones. This is especially handy if you are painting the upper part of a wall or a ceiling.

Drainpipes

The best way to avoid getting paint on the brickwork around a drainpipe is to tape a piece of cardboard behind the pipe. You can hold it there, but it's difficult to hold the cardboard, the paint and the brush all at the same time! When you get to the brace holding the pipe to the wall, and you can't put cardboard behind it, use masking tape on its own.

Drains

Never put tea leaves down the sink: they clog it up. Used coffee grounds on the other hand help keep drains free from grease. Keep your external drains clear by dissolving washing soda in boiling water and pouring it down.

Drawers

If you use a chest of drawers in your workroom or shed, and find that the drawer sometimes slips off the glides, screw an oblong piece of wood vertically to the inside of the back panel. It will stop the drawer being pulled right out – and if you fix it so that it pivots, if you do need to take the drawer out, simply turn the block to the horizontal.

Drilling – 1

To make sure that you don't drill any deeper than you intend to, put masking tape on the drill bit to mark the place where you want to stop drilling. And if you are drilling into a ceiling, keep the dust from raining into your eyes by making a collar from the bottom of an old yoghurt pot and drilling though it.

Drilling – 2

If you are drilling wood, rest the piece you are drilling on a piece of scrap wood. It stops the wood splitting when it breaks through the other side.

Drilling – 3

If you are drilling into a hollow wall and you are not sure where the studs are, run a compass over the wall. The needle will move when the compass passes over a stud and you know not to drill there.

Drills

If you spray your drill bits with a silicone spray before you use them, not only will they stay sharper longer, they will be less likely to break.

Drip tray

Even the most careful of DIY decorators is bound to find that some paint drips and runs down the side of the tin and on to the floor. Find a paper plate that's wider than the paint can, dab a little paint on it and fix the plate to the can. Even if the paint does drip, the plate will catch it.

Extending electrical wire

Never ever botch this together with insulating tape or Sellotape. Even if it's very weak speaker cable, always use a flex connector, which you can buy at any electrical shop. Even the mildest current can cause a fire if the wiring is in the least bit faulty.

Exterior painting – 1

If you are painting the outside of a house, don't let the sunlight fall on the paint as you apply it. Doing so may get the paint hot enough to affect the finish and you could end up with an uneven result. Paint each section as it falls into shadow – the paint will dry naturally.

Exterior painting – 2

Dark colours are not to be recommended for exteriors: they absorb heat much more than light colours with the result that they often blister and flake off and as a result require repainting more often.

Exterior painting – 3

For best results, paint the outside of your house when the temperature outside is more than 50°F and less than 90°F and if you can, do it in Spring when there's less chance of leaves blowing on to your freshly painted surfaces. And don't be too eager to get going in the morning. Let the dew evaporate before you start – and finish in the evening before any dampness sets in.

Exterior painting – 4

In sunny weather, paint the west-facing wall in the morning, the east-facing one in the afternoon and the south wall when it is most in the shade – that way you won't get sunburned and strong sunlight won't affect your paint.

Filling it up

Never fill a car's fuel tank full to the brim in very hot weather. The heat increases the pressure in the fuel tank and it may overflow.

Fuse box

If you still have an old-fashioned fuse box, label each fuse with what's on the circuits they control – lamps, television, etc. If a fuse blows you will know right away which one needs rewiring.

Garden tools

If you have a garage with exposed ceiling joists, screw cross members to the bottom edges of the joists and use the space to store hoes, rakes and any other implements that usually compete for space in your shed.

Glue

Less is best. You can always put more on to something that isn't sticking properly. But it can be difficult to get rid of the excess if you put too much on to start with.

Graceful-looking house

To give your house a more elegant and graceful appearance, paint the doors, shutters and windows and any corner trim a contrasting colour to the walls of the house.

Grease spots

If you have grease spots on wallpaper the chances are that they will come through when you come to re-paper. Get round this by dabbing the spot (or spots) with clear varnish or nail varnish remover. That should keep the spots in their place – invisible under the new paper.

Gutters

Check if your gutters are working by running water along them from a garden hose. If any pools of water form, some of the hangers or brackets may be damaged allowing the gutter to sag and need replacing.

Hammering nails – 1

Protect your fingers from hammer blows by holding nails with a clothes peg for the first few blows, until the nail is well into the wood. You can also push the nail through a thin piece of card and use the card to hold the nail in place as you hammer. When the nail has taken hold, simply rip the card clear.

Hammering nails – 2

Always hold the hammer as far from the head as possible and once the nail is firmly in, swing the hammer from your elbow. The simple laws of leverage dictate that the greater the distance between the source of the energy and the point to where it is applied, the greater the force exerted on the point of application.

Have to have

The most important thing in your toolbox is not your hammer, screwdriver or drill. It's a piece of laminated card with a plumber's and electrician's phone number written on it.

Holding nails

If you have to hold a nail to start it off, do so by taking it between the index and middle finger and hold it against the wood with the back of your hand resting on the wood. That way, if you do miss, the hammer head will land on the fleshy part of your finger, which is much less painful than hitting your thumb or fingernail as you would if you hold the nail in the more conventional manner.

Holes to fill

Larger nails can be filled with newspaper before being plastered over. Nail holes can be filled with toothpaste, tinted with a suitable food colouring. And to fill small nail holes in wallpaper, soften the tip of a matchstick with a matching crayon and plug the hole with it.

How much in the can?

If there is too much left in a used paint can for you to throw away, mark the can on the outside at the paint level inside. You can do this by holding an old pencil between finger and thumb, letting your thumb rest on the rim of the can and holding the pencil so that the tip of the lead is just in the paint and no more. Take it out, reverse your thumb so that it is still resting on the rim but the pencil is on the outside of the can. Make a small mark with the blob of paint on the lead and let it dry (or mark the spot with a suitable pen). When next you need paint that colour, you'll know at a glance if what you have in the can is enough for the job.

Insects

Insects landing on a patch of wall or woodwork or whatever you have just painted can be really fiddly to get off, often necessitating yet another bit of brushing. If you put a drop or two of insect repellent in the paint, it may well keep them at bay.

Insulation – 1

When insulating an attic floor for the first time, lay polyethylene sheeting as a vapour barrier between the joists before laying the insulating material, be it specially-bought from your local DIY store, or simply old blankets.

Insulating – 2

When you are insulating your loft always work from the eaves towards the centre. That way, when you need to cut to fit (as you are sure to) you can work in the area with the most headroom. Start at the middle and working outwards is a guarantee of lost tempers and bad backs.

Keeping on the go

If you are painting a wall or a ceiling, try not to take a break longer than a few minutes. If you stop for even as short a time as quarter of an hour, the chances are you'll leave a line that will be almost impossible to get rid of.

Ladders – 1

Never lean a ladder against a gutter. You could easily damage it. Rather, lean the ladder against a stabilizer fixed to the upper part of your ladder.

Ladders – 2

Never stand on the top of a ladder. Venturing any higher than the second-top step is an invitation for accidents to happen. And always keep your hips within the span of the side rails of the ladder.

Ladders – 3

When climbing up and down a ladder, always use two hands and always face the ladder. Keep your tools in your belt or pocket, or haul them up and down in a bucket with rope attached to the handle, long enough to stretch from the top of the ladder to the ground with some to spare.

Leaky attic

If you find a leak in the attic roof, push a long nail through it to help you find the spot when you go on the roof outside to do a spot of detective work.

Leftover paint

When you have finished a painting job, don't throw out the leftover paint. Store a little in a small tin to be used for any patching up you have to do at a later date. Even if you keep a note of the maker and the shade you used, if you need to buy some more, you could well find that the manufacturer has altered the colour just a little and the new paint doesn't match the old.

Lock 'em up

It's best always to keep your tools under lock and key especially if you have young children. Better safe than sorry.

Loose screws

Remove any annoyingly loose screws, wedge a piece of matchstick into
the hole and screw the offender back in. The match should hold it tightly in place.

Manufacturer's instructions

Follow them to the letter. They know more about their product than you do!

Mark 'em

If you sometimes lend out tools, paint or engrave your initials on the handles. It works both ways: the borrower will know that the tools he has borrowed are yours and you will know that any unmarked tools in your shed or workroom must have been borrowed from someone.

Masking it

If you have fiddly bits of decoration on doors, windows or walls that are a nuisance to cover with masking tape but that you don't want to paint over, cover them with petroleum jelly. The paint won't hold and any streaks will come off with a damp cloth.

Metal tools

You can stop your metal tools from rusting by (a) making sure that you dry them thoroughly after each use and that your shed or workroom is bone dry – difficult (b) oiling them after every use – tedious or (c) storing them in sealed wooden bins with camphor and sawdust.

Mildew

Painting over mildew is a complete waste of time – it comes straight through, so it must be removed before you apply the first coat. Do this by applying a little ordinary household bleach. And don't worry about the smell – it will be lost in the smell of the paint you're using.

Nails

If you are nailing thin wood, try flattening the point of the nail just a little – it stops the wood splitting. If you are nailing thin wood onto thick, always nail through the thinner piece into the thicker and if possible, use nails that are three times longer than the thinner piece. And try not to nail in a straight line along the grain. There is less chance of the wood splitting if you do this.

Old paint

When you do you re-use old paint, strain it through the feet end of an old stocking or tight. Any impurities will be filtered out and the paint will be smooth enough to use right away.

Old shower curtains

Don't throw these away no matter how grotty they have become. Put them in a heavy-duty polythene bag and store them to be used next time you are decorating. They make excellent dust cloths to protect the floor and any furniture too large to put in another room while you work.

Paint brushes – 1

To make paint brushes easier to grip, wrap a piece of reasonably thick foam rubber round the handle. With the brush easier to grip, the job is much less tiring.

Paint brushes – 2

If you are doing a gloss job that is going to take more than a day, you don't have to clean your brush each night. Instead, wrap it tightly in clingfilm and simply clean the brush when the job is done. And if, once you have cleaned it, you slip an elastic band over the bristles and leave it there until you next need the brush, your brushes will stay in tip-top condition for much longer.

Paint on hands

If you find it takes ages to get paint off your hands after a DIY session, try rubbing a little petroleum jelly on your hands before you start next time. It seals the pores and makes the paint come off much easier.

Paint skin

The best way to stop a skin forming on the top of gloss paint when you have finished a job, is to pour a thin layer of White Spirit onto the paint before you close the lid. When you come to open it again, simply stir it into the paint. Another way is to store used paint cans upside down. When you turn it back to open it, any skin will be at the bottom of the can.

Paint smell

Put half an onion, cut side up, on a plate in the room you are painting. It takes most of the smell of the paint away.

Paint stirrer

A wire coat hanger (see Wiping brushes below) makes a more than adequate paint stirrer – much better than the handle of an old spoon or piece of wood.

Paint trays

Always line a paint tray with aluminium foil before using it. When the job is finished, throw away the foil and the tray is as good as new for next time. Or, you can slip it into a plastic bag turned inside-out. When the job is done, just peel the bag off and you can put the tray away without having to wash it.

Painting a room

Try to work uninterrupted for three or four hours at a stretch. This allows you to work in consistent light and you should be able to get the first coat on in an average-size room in that time.

Painting ceilings – 1

If you are painting your ceiling to cover up a water stain, don't use emulsion: the stain will come through it no matter how many coats you apply. Use a matte oil based paint to cover the stain.

Painting ceilings – 2

To stop paint dripping down your arm next time you are painting a ceiling, go to your local vet and buy the smallest flea-collar he stocks. Tape it securely to your paintbrush and even if the paint does drip, it won't run down your arm. You can also cut a suitably shaped and sized hole in the middle of a paper plate and push your brush through it, but the cat's flea collar can be less cumbersome.

Painting drainpipes

When painting drainpipes or other circular objects, work diagonally at first from the top downwards and finish with long strokes along its length. You'll get much better coverage that way.

Painting furniture

When painting a piece of furniture, stand each leg in a jam jar to catch any drips.

Painting over wallpaper

If you HAVE to do this (it really is best to scrape the paper off and put on a decent lining paper before painting a room) always paint a sample patch in an unseen part of the room. Above the skirting board behind the door, or under the window where it will be hidden by the curtain are the best places. Why? Because some wallpapers will bleed colour through emulsion paint which can be difficult to cover.

Painting radiators

When painting radiators, use special non-metallic paint for the task. Metallic paints absorb heat so radiators painted with it will not be as warm, and your heating bill may rise.

Painting railings

The two things you need when painting railings – apart from the paint – are a length of cardboard to put behind them, and a paint spray. Using a brush is fiddly, time-consuming and extremely boring.

Painting round wall fittings

If you have wall light fittings, cover each one with a polythene bag and secure it with an elastic band at open end. Any drips and splashes will be caught on the bags and you won't have to spend hours cleaning paint from splattered-covered fittings.

Painting roofs

If you paint any metal roof flashing the same colour as your roof, it will make it much less noticeable.

Painting stairs

In order to be able to use stairs when painting them, paint alternate treads, letting the paint dry, then painting the ones that are left. That way, you can go up and down the staircase, taking the stairs two at a time.

Painting windows

Always leave sash cords made of natural material unpainted when painting a window. The paint eats into the cord and makes it fray – and replacing a window sash cord is not the easiest of tasks.

Papering round light sockets

When papering round square light sockets paper over them first then very, very carefully cut two diagonals, corner to corner and trim. Wait until the paste dries and you will have a really neat finish.

Picture hooks

Fixing a cross of masking tape on the wall where you intend knocking in a picture hook will stop the plaster from cracking.

Plaster

When you are mixing plaster, always add plaster to water, never water to plaster. You are less likely to get lumps if you do this. And if your plaster is drying too quickly, add a little vinegar to the mix.

Plastering

If you have a large hole to fill with plaster, do it layer by layer, allowing each layer to dry thoroughly before applying the next. If you fill it in one go, the filler won't take properly.

Power-tool cables

Keep them out of harm's way when you are working with electric tools on your workbench by hooking the slack on a spring of suitable length screwed into the ceiling directly above your workbench.

Removing nails

When you are using a claw hammer to remove a nail from a piece of wood, protect the surface by slipping a thin piece of scrap wood or rubber under the hammer head. Otherwise you may scratch or dent the wood.

Repairing round objects

When you have glued the broken edges of a round object together, hold them in place with an elastic band: not too tight, or else the repaired vessel may implode! Never drink out of a cup that has been repaired, or eat off a plate that has been broken and glued back together. No matter how well you wash them, the cracks will always harbour germs and bacteria.

Right order

When painting a room it's ceiling first and then – in order – walls and alcoves, doors, windows, skirting boards and radiators. If you're painting the ceiling and papering the walls and alcoves, it's ceiling then doors etc, leaving papering the walls and any alcoves to the end.

Rubber gloves

Don't wear rubber gloves when you painting – it's difficult to grip the can tightly enough to prevent it slipping through your fingers.

Rusty bolts

If a bolt has rusted and is proving hard to move, try pouring some fizzy drink over it then wiping it clean.

Sawing

There's less chance of thin wood splintering as you saw if you position the wood so that the growth rings arc downwards. Always start with a few short strokes, pulling the saw towards you before starting to use longer, more powerful strokes, pressing down on the push strokes and relaxing as you pull the saw back towards you.

Sawing circles

If you are using an electric saw to cut a circle out of a piece of plywood, make straight cuts from the edge of the wood to the circumference of the circle, lining up with the diameter, every 30 degrees. As you saw, the waste wood falls off in sections, cutting the stress on the blade and making it less likely that the wood will split.

Sawing knots

When you come to a knot in the wood, change the angle of the blade as you saw, making it more flush to the wood.

Sawing metal

If you are using a hacksaw to saw through metal, use a file to start off the kerf (see Tight sawing) with a file. It gives you a groove to position the saw and makes it much less likely to slip.

Saws

Saws work more efficiently and you will save yourself a lot of elbow work if you rub the blade with a little dry soap before you start. It reduces the friction and less friction means less work.

Screwing

Try to ensure that the tip of the screwdriver you plan to use is as close to the width and length of the slot in the screw. If the tip is too narrow, you may damage the slit, making it hard to take the screw out should you ever need to. If it's too wide, the screwdriver may slip and scratch the wood.

Screws – 1

To keep screws firmly in position once you have screwed them in, dab a little clear nail varnish under the head before tightening them completely. It keeps the screws where you want them but offers little or no resistance when you come to unscrew them.

Screws – 2

If you have to get a screw into a hard-to-reach place, before you start push the screw through a slit of masking tape with the adhesive side up, put the screwdriver in the screw's slit and fold the tape up, sticking the sides together to hold the screw in position on the screwdriver.

Screws – 3

If a screw is proving particularly hard to turn or tighten, unscrew it and rub some soap or paraffin into the thread. It should go in much more easily. Dipping them into petroleum jelly makes them easier to remove later.

Self-sticking hooks

Coat the sticky side with clear nail varnish before putting them in place – somehow they're never as sticky as you think they are going to be!

Sharp tools

Next time you buy a large electrical appliance that comes wrapped in polystyrene, cut a suitably-sized piece, line the bottom of an appropriate container and use it to store your sharp tools in – points embedded in the polystyrene.

Small saws

Cut a piece of old garden hose, make a slit in it and use it as protection for the teeth of your small handsaws. For larger saws, protect the teeth with a suitably sized piece of the inner tube of an old car tyre.

Smelly paint

If the smell of fresh paint makes you feel nauseous, a teaspoon of vanilla essence in a half-litre can of paint will neutralize at least some, if not all, of the paint smell without affecting the colour.

Snow on roofs

If the snow on part of a roof regularly melts before the rest, it could mean that the insulation in the loft is damaged. Go up into the attic and give it the once-over.

Storing nails

That the best things in which to store nails, nuts and bolts, screws and the like is are old screw-top jam and mayonnaise jars. To double your shelf space glue the lids to the underside of suitable shelves – using an appropriate super glue – and screw the storage jars, upwards, into them.

Squeaky floorboards

Try sprinkling talcum powder or French chalk around the joints. Either one usually stops floorboards from squeaking.

Stripping paint from wood

Never use a blowtorch when stripping paint from wood that is going to be left unpainted. You could leave scorch marks.

Stripping wallpaper

Next time you have wallpaper to scrape off, go to the chemist and buy some alum. Dissolve two teaspoons for every pint of warm water in your bucket. Wet the paper thoroughly with a brush or a roller and after it has dried in, you should find that the wallpaper comes off easily.

Tight sawing

First a word you may not have heard before – kerf: it's the channel made by the blade of a saw. And if your handsaw is sticking as you saw, insert a screwdriver into the kerf to hold it open.

Tight screws

If a screw is proving too tight to get out, try heating the tip of your screwdriver.

Tightening up

If you are having difficulty getting screws as tight as you would like them, drill a hole through the handle of your screwdriver and slip a long nail through it. Using this should give you the extra leverage you need.

Tiling

Never tile over wallpaper. If the wallpaper comes off the wall, the tiles come with it.

Tools

Always put tools back in their proper place, even if you are just taking a tea break. Stick to this rule and you will save hours of frustrating searches and rummaging through toolboxes wondering where you have put the thing.

Touch-up repairs

After you have finished a painting job, fill an empty (and clean) nail-varnish jar with some of the paint you have used. With the brushes built in to the handles, they are great for covering up any scratches or flakes.

Washing hands

If white spirit chaps your hands when you wash them after painting and the chemical proprietary hand washes are too strong, try rubbing a knob of butter or olive oil into your hands and then washing it off with warm, soapy water. As often as not the paint come off easily.

Wallpaper – 1

When buying wallpaper, don't be afraid to take the samples book out of the shop and into natural light. Always take a sheet of neutral coloured paper with you against which to view your preliminary choices. If you view them against a coloured background, you may well end up regretting your final choice when the paper is hung.

Wallpaper – 2

Large areas of a single colour tend to concentrate the colour and may make it sigficantly different from the shade you had in mind when you made your choice. It's always best to select a slightly paler shade then you have in mind when buying your wallpaper.

Wallpaper – 3

If, despite your best efforts, your freshly dried wallpapered wall looks like a lunar landscape, find a syringe and fill it with paste. Inject it into the blisters and wait until the paper has absorbed the paste before gently flattening them. When you have injected them all, very carefully run a roller over the wall, and with any luck it will be as flat as a croquet lawn.

Wallpaper – 4

You could make a note of the number of rolls it takes to paper a room and put it somewhere safe. Otherwise write it on a thin piece of pasted paper and stick it to the top of the door frame.

Wallpapering – 5

Unless you are a dab hand at this, buy a spare roll. Work out how many rolls you need and buy a spare one. Accidents can happen when you are hanging the paper, and it's better to have a spare roll to hand rather than having to stop work and go and buy some more. And if you have to effect a repair at a later stage, you may find that the paper you used has been discontinued.

Wallpaper paste

Next time you are wallpapering, pour the paste into a paint tray and use a roller to apply it to the paper. The paste spreads easily and in a fraction of the time it takes with a brush.

White spirit

We all clean our brushes with white spirit then empty the jar down the sink. Don't. If you keep the liquid for a few days, the paint will sink to the bottom leaving clean spirit above. Carefully drain this off into a clean bottle and put it in the shed, cupboard, attic or wherever you keep your DIY stuff.

Windows

Masking tape is all very well, but if you forget to take it off right away, it can be a difficult to remove. Better to keep the glass free of paint by covering it with damp strips of newspaper, which will stay in place long enough for you to paint the frame – and it comes off in a flash.

If you do get paint on the glass and it's still fresh, it can be removed with a solution of three parts warm water to one part vinegar. If it's hardened, you'll have to scrape it off – a single-edged razor blade is ideal, but do be careful.

Wiping brushes

Forget the rag that most DIY painters use to wipe their brushes as they go. Find a pair of wirecutters and a wire coat hanger. Cut a length long enough to be wound round the lid end of the can stretched right across the diameter of the open can with enough left over to be twisted round the can again and secured tightly. Make sure the twisted end is well tucked in and that you won't catch your hand on it.

Wiring

The way to remember which wire goes where when wiring a plug used to be BRown = Bottom Right, BLue = Bottom Left and the one left, the earth, to the pin at the top. Now the word to remember is BuGgeR – Blue to the left, Green/yellow straight up and Red to the right.

Workroom or shed essential...

... a magnet – ideal for picking up dropped nails, screws, and other small metal bits and pieces that are difficult to pick up with the fingers.

Workroom storage

An old bathroom cabinet fixed to the back of your shed or workroom door is a great place to store screws, nails and small tools like screwdrivers and drill bits.

Practical
Household Hints

Gardening – indoors and out

You can hardly switch on a television programme these days without some enthusiastic, green-fingered expert exhorting you to get out there and garden. If you can't beat them...

Ageing

If you want to age a piece of garden furniture paint it with natural yoghurt. It encourages mosses and algae to grow and gives an almost-instant weathered look. Liquid manure also does the trick.

Ants

This may sound eccentric but it does work. Next time you see columns of ants in the garden or house, put some ordinary two pence pieces in their way. They leave – quickly.

Bananas

Lay banana skins into a hole before planting a rose, or line a trench in which you are going to plant vegetables. The skins rot quickly and nourish the soil with calcium, magnesium, sulphur, phosphates, sodium and silica. You can also put some banana skins in your compost heap – they speed up the composting process.

Birds

Keep birds away from precious crops by stretching the tape from the inside of broken music cassettes between suitably spaced posts. The tape vibrates in the breeze and makes a sound that deters birds.

Bottomless pots

Some pots, including artificial chimney pots, often come bottomless and the plants put in them are liable to attack from insect pests. You can stop this by standing the pots on a piece of fine-gauge wire mesh or a piece from an old net curtain.

Bracken

Unless you are planting plants that like lime, put a handful of roughly cut-up bracken into the hold before you put the plant it. It improves the texture of the soil and gives the plant an extra little boost.

Bulbs

Always squeeze bulbs before you buy them and if they feel in the least bit hollow or in any way not firm, put them back. If you're on good terms with your nurseryman, tell him what you're doing. And if you can't plant them right away, store your bulbs in a cool, dry place until you can – but don't leave it too long.

Buying plants

Never buy a perennial if it's wilting. Best to choose a healthy specimen in compost that is not too wet and not too dry. Don't buy plants if the pot is cracked – the roots may be damaged, too. And if there's even a suspicion of moss, weeds or liverworts, give the pot a wide berth.

Cats

Cats hate the smell of oranges, so if you sprinkle some finely chopped orange peel around your garden they will stay clear of it. They also don't like getting their paws prickled, so if you push some rose prunings or holly leaves into the soil, they will stay away. Another trick is to scatter mothballs on the flowerbeds.

Climbers

To give your climbers a wilder, more natural look, train some new growth back unevenly. Doing this also makes a newly planted climber look more established than it is.

Compost

The best compost containers have a removable front panel to allow easy access. This makes regular turning easier and also makes it easier to get at when you want to remove some to spread in the garden – making sure that the compost is well rotted first.

Brick edging

Edge paths by digging a small trench along both sides and laying bricks in it so that each one rests on the point of one corner, supported by the neighbouring brick. When you have finished brick laying, pack soil tightly round the bricks and you have a secure, attractive edging that will last for years.

Bulbs – 1

Plant bulbs at a depth of two-and-a-half times their diameter. Any shallower and they'll come up too early, any deeper and they may not come through at all. So if your daffs are 7.5 centimetres in diameter, plant them just under 19 centimetres deep and you should have a host of golden daffodils come spring.

Bulbs – 2

If you have a wood-burning stove and the soil in your garden isn't too acid, save the ashes during the growing season and sprinkle them over where you planted your bulbs. The wood ash increases the soils acidity and encourages your bulbs to bear bigger and longer-lasting blooms.

Bulbs – 3

If snowdrops and crocuses add splashes of welcome colour to your lawn in early spring, let the bulb foliage die back before you give the lawn it's first cut in that area. It's a great source of nourishment for next year's blooms.

Bulbs – 4

If you planted bulbs indoors for winter colour, don't waste your time and effort planting them outside, hoping they will grow in the garden next season. They won't.

Clean leaves

Cut old supermarket bags into suitable shapes and sizes and use them to cover the soil in your plant pots before putting them in the shower and running lukewarm water over them for a moment or two. The leaves love it and will come out gleamingly clean. Or, on a clammy, muggy day when there's a shower, put your indoor plants in the rain for a minute or two. But don't do either of these with plants with hairy leaves.

Climbing roses

You don't have to use climbing roses to ramble up trellis, pergolas and the like. They make beautiful ground cover, too. All you have to do is peg their canes to the ground with wire hoops and they will grow a treat. Great for covering anything that's flat and unsightly.

Cold tea

Most plants love cold tea and thrive on it. Try it.

Crocking plant pots

Many experts suggest putting pieces of broken flowerpots in new ones before adding the potting compost. Excess water drains into them and stops the roots getting waterlogged. Even better is to crock your pots with broken eggshells. Not only do they serve the same purpose, they enrich the compost or earth with calcium and help keep plants healthy.

Cut your heating bills

If you plant a shield of a double row of evergreen trees or large shrubs on the side of the house facing the prevailing wind, they will keep the wind out and your winter fuel heating bill down.

Cuttings

If you are a keen flower arranger and use oasis for your displays, you can reuse it to pot shrub cuttings. Insert the seedlings into the wet oasis, and when the roots appear, pot the seedlings up in the usual way, in suitable growing compost.

Delicate plants

If you have an especially delicate plant that needs special watering, dip a sponge in tepid water and squeeze it over the pot. Even the most delicate of plants won't object to such gentle treatment.

Digging tools

Keep a tub of sand mixed with old motor oil – twenty kilos of sand to a litre of oil – and plunge the blades of your digging tools into it three or four times after you use them. It cleans and lubricates them simultaneously.

Division time

Let your eyes be the judge of the best place to divide a plant. Look for the place where you will do least harm to the plant, then feel around a bit to establish the exact spot to do the deed.

Dogs

Discourage dogs from crawling under your fence by planting pyracantha or a similar prickly shrub at their entry points. They soon get the message.

Double harvest

When spring-planted cabbage is about the size of a small football harvest them, leaving the four outer leaves on each stalk. Come autumn, there will be one small but delicious cabbage for each of the leaves you left.

Double-purpose screen

If you want to screen the compost heap or an unkempt part of the garden out of sight, plant sunflowers round it and grow runner beans up the stems. Not only do you have an attractive screen, the beans add density and are a ready source of fresh vegetables.

Earwigs

If these garden pests are making a meal of your young plants, roll some damp newspaper into a roll and leave it by the where the bugs have been at work. Next morning it will be full of the little blighters.

Easy watering

When you dig a hole to put a plant in, lay a length of rubber tubing or drainpipe into it, one end open on the surface of the soil. When the plant needs watering, simply pour some down the tube and the roots will benefit hugely and the plant will flourish.

Eyesores

If you have an eyesore in your garden that while not impossible to remove is going to be difficult – a post sunk in concrete for instance – use it to support a suitable climber, either planted into the soil around the offending item or in an attractive pot alongside it.

Fishponds

When the weather turns cold and it looks like a frost is in the air, fill a plastic bottle with hot water and float it in your garden pond. Should the pond freeze over, the water around the bottle should stay unfrozen and there will be no danger of your fish suffocating though lack of oxygen. If you live in an area where herons make a meal of pond fish, cut both ends off some plastic bottles and lay the remaining tubes on the bottom of the pond, keeping them in place with some gravel. Should the herons swoop, the fish can swim to safety into the plastic refuge.

Eggshells

Don't throw used eggshells away. Keep them in a screw-top jar filled with cold water and use it to water your houseplants.

Fenceposts

Fenceposts will shed water more effectively and last longer if you saw off the tops at an angle, or fit them with a decorative, pointed (but not too sharp) metal cap, which should be available at your garden centre.

Flotsam free

If twigs and other debris run down the pipe into your water butt, you can stop this by stretching some old tights over the bottom of the downpipe and securing them with an strong rubber band. Remember to clean it regularly especially after it has been raining heavily.

Flowerpots

A used teabag in the bottom of a flowerpot stops the soil falling through the draining hole and as a bonus is good drainage. To eke out potting compost, crumble up some polystyrene and put it up to a quarter of the depth of the pot. Not only does it save on compost, it's great drainage, too.

Frosty weather

During the winter cut the tops and bottoms off plastic lemonade bottles and press the remaining cylinder into the soil around plants that need special protection from the frost. And if you sprinkle sea salt onto garden paths and drives, it should stop them freezing over. And never walk on frosty grass: you'll damage it and make it susceptible to some diseases.

Fruit thieves

To stop squirrels and birds attacking your fruit before you have a chance to pick them, buy some cheap aluminium plates, puncture a hole in them and tie them close together to the lower branches of the trees. It may look odd, but as the plates clang in the breeze, greedy pests will be scared off.

Garden canes

To be safe, put an empty yoghurt or the top of a fabric conditioner bottle, a small potato or the fingers of an old pair of rubber gloves over the end of each cane. It makes them much easier to see.

Gardening mat

If your gardening mat has seen better days and your knees aren't up to kneeling on the grass with nothing underneath, a rubber hot water bottle stuffed with old tights makes an ideal and comfortable substitute.

Garlic and the indoor gardener

Save the skins when peeling garlic and put them around the compost of your houseplants, especially those in your conservatory.

Whitefly hate garlic and will give even the merest whiff of it a wide berth. And if you bury a clove of garlic in a plantpot, you are unlikely to see even a single greenfly on any of your plants.

Germinating seeds

Pouring boiling water on soil before planting seeds that are known to be reluctant to germinate often gets them off to a good start. Sow the seed when the soil has cooled but is still warm and cover with a cloche made by cutting the largest plastic bottle you can find, down the middle from neck to base.

Greenfly

If greenfly are getting at your pot plants and hanging baskets, next time you plant them add a French marigold. The greenfly don't like marigolds at all and will give the containers a wide berth. And if they have been feasting on your roses, plant a clove of garlic at the base of each rose bush.

Greenhouse warmer

If you have an unheated greenhouse with no electricity you can protect your precious plants from really severe frosts by burning candles under inverted terracotta plant pots.

Growbags

If you would rather not spend your money on growbags, but still want to give your cuttings a good start, make your own for a fraction of what they cost in garden centres and ironmongers. All you need are suitably sized plastic carrier bags and a bag of cheap compost. Fill the bags with the compost and water it well before putting the plants in. This is especially useful for bringing on plants that like to grow in their own containers.

Handcare

Gardening can play havoc with the hands, especially for those who find wearing gardening gloves restrictive. If that is the case, keep your nails clean by scraping them over a bar of soap before you start. When you have finished, simply hold your hands under running hot water – the soap comes out easily, leaving spotlessly clean nails. If your hands are a bit rough and you're out of handcream, add a teaspoon of sugar to a teaspoon of olive oil, rub in and wash.

Hanging baskets

Hanging basket chains can be heavy and unsightly. Train trailing plants up them to cover them up. Wind them gently round the metal links or thread them through, securing them with green twine or plastic ties.

Hawthorn hedges

If your hawthorn hedge has become a bit straggly and sparse-looking, bend some of the more pliable stems back and peg them into the soil with small metal hooks. Within a week or two, some if not all of them will have taken root and soon the base of the hedge will be looking full and healthy again.

Hedge trimmers

Accidents can happen, so fix two metres of flexible, plastic tubing over the electric cable at the trimmer end of a hedge trimmer. Should the cable slip between the blades, the cable won't get cut and there will be no danger of electrocution.

Hostas

If you like hostas and cultivate them on your patio or conservatory, make sure that they don't suffer from the unwelcome attention of slugs by smearing Vaseline all the way round ten centimetres down from the rim.

Hot stuff

Next time you are cooking with chilli peppers save the seeds and put them somewhere warm to dry. Then plant them in some compost along with some of the coriander seeds you use for cooking. It won't be long before you have bunches of fresh

coriander and chilli plants, with their attractive white flowers, to
hand whenever you need them.

Instant flowerbed

If you grow tomato plants in gro-bags, put them in the garden
when there's no danger of frost and surround them with a wall
made of old bricks. When the tomatoes can be put in pots in the
greenhouse, tip the soil from the bags into the new bed and plant
spring bulbs in it.

Insulating your pots

Before you plant up potted plants destined for the patio, terrace or
somewhere else out of doors, line the sides (not the bottom) with
bubble wrap. It prevents the compost and the rootball being
adversely affected by winter frosts.

Leatherjackets

If you see starlings feasting on your lawn, you could well have
leatherjackets in the grass. Get rid of them by watering the lawn
and covering it with black polythene. Next morning, when you roll
the polythene back, you should find that the grubs stuck to it.

Lime tester

Check the lime content of your soil by dropping a little of it into a
jar of vinegar. If the vinegar starts to bubble, there's plenty of lime
in your soil. If there are no bubbles, lime the soil with 100 grams
lime to every square metre.

Marrows

When your marrows are starting to ripen, keep them out of danger
from the attention of birds by wrapping them in old tights or
stockings. Pull the leg over one end of each marrow and tie it
securely at the other.

Manure

Cow and horse manure can give off ammonia and if used fresh may well scorch your plants. Best to store it for up to year in a covered heap or in closed bags. Once it's rotted, spread it among your ornamental plants as a mulch or top dressing or dig in into your vegetables apart from root ones. Their long roots will feed on the manure instead of going deep into the soil where you want them to go.

Mint

If you are planting a tub or bed with lots of herbs, always plant mint in its pot. This restricts its pot growth and will stop it swamping the other herbs you put in with it.

Moles

Moles create havoc in a garden. If you can find the entrance to their tunnel you can get rid of them by pouring the oil from a can of sardines down it. They also dislike the smell of orange peel and mothballs.

Moving perennials

Autumn or spring are the best times for moving or dividing perennials, but if you have to do this in the summer, do so on a cool day and water it well beforehand. Try to move the plant just before dark, so that it has time to recover during the night, and will not be subjected to the heat of the midday sun.

Muddy boots

If you have to go indoors for any reason during a gardening session, leave a pair of shower caps at the back door. Slip them over your shoes when you go inside and kick them off when you come back into the garden. At the end of the gardening, simply turn them inside out and run the mud on the inside off under a tap.

Mulching

Old carpets make great mulch! Cut a square or circle of carpet slightly larger than the root system and make a slit in it to enable you to put the carpet round the plant. When you've done, cover the carpet with a thin layer of chipped bark or soil.

Neat edges

If you are lucky enough to come across a builders skip with some broken, interlocking clay roof tiles lurking in a corner, ask if you can have them and use them to edge your flowerbeds. Inserted vertically around a circular flowerbed, they look great.

Netting

If you use nets to protect your vegetables and fruits, check them regularly to ensure that no birds or small mammals have become trapped in them. And if there are, put on a pair of stout gloves before trying to free them. A panicky bird can give you a nasty peck and many small mammals have very sharp teeth.

Newspaper mulch

A layer of old newspaper several sheets thick, anchored with rock is terrific mulch. It's cheap, it conserves water and it's bio-degradable. But only use the black and white section – coloured ink may contain lead and damage the plants.

Old hosepipe

Some birds and cats steer well clear of snakes. A suitable length of old hose pipe laid in the cabbage patch or wherever can fool some garden pests into thinking there's a serpent in the garden and keep them away.

Oversprinkling

Overwatering a lawn can be as bad for it as letting it dry out. If you use a sprinkler, put a straight-sided jam jar about a metre from the sprinkler head. When the water level in the jar reaches about 2.5 centimetres, it's time to move the sprinkler to another part of the lawn.

Parsley

If you are growing parsley from seed pour some boiling water on the seeds before you sow them. It speeds up germination and you can thin the young plants out much more quickly.

Plant protectors

If you are using weedkiller to zap the weeds in a path or border, protect the plants you want to survive by putting a cardboard box or polythene bin liner over them.

Plastic containers

Plastic pots are much better than terracotta ones for young plants: they're much easier to clean properly, and less likely to harbour pests, unlike wooden trays and clay pots which are porous.

Pollen beetles

Cut flowers can sometimes become infested with these little pests. Get rid of them by giving the flowers a good shake and standing them overnight in a dark shed or garage with one light left on. The attraction the light has for the beetles is stronger than the appeal of their floral home and they will head for it, leaving your flowers pest-free.

Poisonous plants

Always label poisonous plants very clearly – not just with the name, but with the reaction that it causes when swallowed or brushed against and the action that should be taken in such an event. This is especially important if children are allowed in the garden.

Pricking seedlings

This sometimes-tiresome task can be made much easier if you use a golf tee as a dibber.

Pruning roses

How much to prune, that's the question. Everyone you ask seems to have their own opinion. Dead, damaged and any diseased wood should be cut away. Then get rid of all branches that are criss-crossing and any that look a bit puny. Always wear stout gardening gloves when pruning roses. You can't do the job properly with unprotected hands.

Rattling fences

If the wind rattles your garden fence, wedge the loose struts with old wine bottle corks cut lengthways, diagonally.

Retaining walls

Unfortunately, retaining walls don't allow excess water to drain from the soil. You can get round this by leaving a few of the lower joints free of mortar and keeping the resulting 'weep hole' free of debris.

Roses

Next time you plant roses, add some roughly chopped banana skins to the soil. Not only will the roses enjoy the potassium they provide, they improve the texture of the soil and increase water retention.

Rubble

Disguise rubble with a climber such as a rose or clematis and make a feature of it. It will save you the back-breaking task of lugging bricks into a skip. One caveat though: if there is any concrete in the rubble, don't use a plant that doesn't like lime.

Runner beans

Fresh runner beans are one of the joys of summer. When choosing seeds for planting, drop each one into a jar of water and discard those that float. Planting only those that sink straight to the bottom should guarantee a bumper crop.

Saplings

Protect your saplings from the unwanted attentions of rabbits, mice and other pests by wrapping the trunks in fibreglass insulation, and keeping it there until the young tree is well established.

Save water

During the summer when there are often appeals to save water,

move some of your container plants to under any hanging baskets
you have. When you water the basket, the overflow will water the
plants below. Not only do you save water, you save on liquid feed,
too.

Seeds

If you are going to save the seeds from Love-lies-bleeding or any
other heavily laden small-seeded plants that tend to drop their
seeds, tie a paper back round the seed head for a week or two
before you intend collecting the seeds. It's a good idea to do this
with onions, too.

Shovelling snow

Before you start this often back-breaking task, melt a candle over
the shovel. This gives it an instant, if temporary, non-stick coating
which the snow slides off easily.

Slugs – 1

Next time you are enjoying a can of beer, leave a few drops in the
can, widen the hole and leave it on its side in the garden. Slugs love
beer so will crawl in and drown. You can also bury yoghurt pots up
to their tops, fill them with beer and in a day or two you'll have a
potful of slugs. If the little perishers have been feasting on your
runner beans (and you are reluctant to use poisonous slug pellets)
put some old eggshells in the oven, bake them for a few minutes,
crush them and sprinkle them around the plants.

Slugs – 2

If you have just planted some seedlings out and are worried about
them being ravaged by slugs, sprinkle some bran around them. Not
only does it keep the slugs away, it's harmless to birds and others
unlike some slug pellets. Another way is to surround the plants with
holly leaves. It may not kill the slugs, but it does keep them away.

Small garden produce

Having a small garden shouldn't stop you growing fruit –

occasionally. There is no reason why you can't plant fruit and vegetables among your flowers – chives, parsley and strawberries make neat borders and the fronds of carrots and asparagus look lovely planted among perennials.

Soil types

A simple test to find out more about the kind of soil you have is take small handful of it between your fingers and try to roll it into a ball. If it won't stick together, you probably have light, sandy soil. If it feels gritty but does form a ball, the chances are you have a handful of lime. If it's sticky and takes a shine when rub your thumb over it, then you have clay.

Spike it

Wear old golf shoes when you mow the lawn. The spikes loosen and aerate the soil beneath the grass and keep it healthy. If you are not a golfer, most garden centres now sell spiked shoes for this purpose.

Storing bulbs

When the time comes that flowering bulbs are finished and should be taken out, store them in old tights. You will be surprised at how many bulbs an about-to-be-discarded pair of ripped tights can hold: and you can hang them from a hook or a nail in the garden shed or a cupboard indoors.

Storing seeds

If you are saving seeds to plant next season, pour them into small film canisters. They don't take up much room, they're watertight (handy in case of accidents in the shed), airtight and they are easy to label and date with a small sticky label.

Single seeds

If you are sewing seeds singly rather than scattering them to be thinned out later, find a box of matches, some old egg boxes and your potting compost. Fill each half-egg hole with compost, damp the end of a match and use it to pick each seed up one by one and plant it. The task complete, you can plant the box directly into the soil.

Snails

Dig some old half-coconut shells, cut side up into your flowerbeds. Snails will fall into them and find themselves unable to get out. Slugs and woodlice will be similarly trapped.

Spotlights

If you are planning to highlight garden features such as statue or an ornamental pond with a spot or floodlight, remember the neighbours and make sure that the light won't affect them in any way.

Stopping squashing

When you are watering the garden, it's hard to avoid the hosepipe dragging over a flowerbed and squashing some of the plants. You can stop this from happening by banging some short wooden stumps into the corner of each bed, or if it is a particularly long one, at regular intervals along the edge.

Storing plants

If the plants you bring home from the nursery have bare roots, store them in an unheated garage or shed for a few days, the roots covered with old hessian sacking or polythene to prevent them drying out.

Sweetpeas – 1

Make small, suitably sized tubes of newspaper, secure them with tape and fill them with compost. They make ideal individual containers for sweetpeas or other flowers grown from seeds, and can be planted directly into the garden without taking the seedlings out as the newspaper will decompose naturally.

Sweetpeas – 2

Speed up the germinating period of these summer favourites by putting them between two polystyrene trays lined with moist tissue or kitchen paper in a sealed plastic bag. The seeds should germinate within a week at the most.

Teabags

Don't throw old teabags away. Use them to line the bottom of your plant pots. They are excellent drainage – much better than the traditional crocks and easier to recycle.

Tight ties

Cut the legs of old tights and stockings into strips and use them to tie rose bushes and other plants to fences, walls, stakes and canes. As the plants grow, the material stretches and shouldn't have to be replaced during the lifetime of the plant. And if the ties do happen to break, by that time the plant should be able to stand on its own roots.

Tools

Are you are the sort of gardener who is always misplacing tools in a herbaceous border and whose garden shed is a jumble of identically coloured handles sticking out of a row of old cardboard boxes? If so, paint them all different, bright colours and stick a list as to which is which on the inside of the shed door. If you should lose them in a border, you'll find them more easily. And if you're looking for a spade, simply consult the list and look for the correctly coloured handle.

Trees

If you are planting a new shrub tree, especially a water-loving one like a willow or ornamental fig, keep it well away from drains and, if you have one, your septic tank. As they grow, the roots can damage the piping or casing and cause rather smelly damage.

Trellis divider

Even small gardens can be given a new lease of life if you divide it into two distinct parts, front and back. Do this by putting a trellis arch half way down the garden, planting climbers around it and a screen of evergreens on either side. It's amazing how easy it is to give each part its own distinct character by using different plants and using separate planting schemes in both halves.

Turf repairs

If part of your lawn develops a hollow because of heavy use, cut a deep cross over the area you want to even out, carefully peel back the turf sections and fill the hollow with top soil mixed with some finely chopped-up old car tyre. Not only is the hollow filled, but the rubber makes the area resilient to future pounding.

Vines

If you live in the warm south or have a conservatory and grow vines, when it comes to cutting them back cut the prunings just below a bud, into short lengths. Put them in a jar of water on a windowsill that gets the sun and when the roots appear pot them up.

Vinyl hoses

Never keep vinyl hoses anywhere they will be in the sun for any length of time – the ultraviolet rays deteriorates the vinyl and it will soon start to leak.

Weed barrier

If there is any danger of roots from your neighbours' gardens creeping under a fence and into your garden, dig a trench 30cm deep on your side of the fence and line it with heavy-duty polythene then replace the soil.

Weeds

Strong, chemical weedkillers are still popular with some gardeners, especially for getting rid of weeds that are growing in awkward and difficult-to-get-to nooks and crannies. But those who prefer not to use chemicals can kill weeds by pouring boiling water over them. If they prove resistant to that, sprinkle salt or bicarbonate of soda on them. Salt it also good at getting rid of dandelions: pour some on the leaves and it dries them up and kills them within the week. And if you have moss on your drive, dissolve some washing soda in boiling water and pour it on.

Weevils

Stop weevils laying their eggs in greenhouse pot plants by applying a narrow circle of non-setting glue around them. Weevils can't fly and have to crawl to their destination. The glue stops them.

Wheelbarrows

Before you start to fill your wheelbarrow, point it in the direction you're going to wheel it.

Windowboxes

If you live in a flat, check your lease before putting window boxes on your ledges. Some leases have clauses either banning window boxes or making it necessary to seek the landlord's permission. Also, check your insurance. Should an accident happen and the window box dislodges and falls on someone below, you are responsible and could well find yourself being sued for damages.

Worktable

If you are potting flowers or filling hanging baskets in the garden, use an old ironing board as a work table. It saves you bending and can be easily collapsed and carried from one part of the garden to another.

Practical Household Hints

Health and beauty

Beauty comes from within, so if you keep yourself healthy, half the battle to looking great is already won!

Acne

If your children are going through the pimple stage, add two tablespoonfuls of white vinegar to a cup of water that has been boiled but has cooled down a bit. Wash the face thoroughly and then apply the solution to the affected area. Don't expect a flawless complexion overnight, but after a day or two you will see a big improvement.

Alcohol

Look upon alcohol, especially spirits, as an occasional friend rather than a bosom buddy and you'll be, and look, all the better for it. And at drinks parties, if you alternate each drink with a glass of water, you won't regret it in the morning.

Anaemia

Steam a large handful of nettle tops until they are tender, add two teaspoons of honey and eat as a vegetable with your main meal of the day. Don't worry about stinging your mouth – the cooking takes the sting out of the nettle.

Anxiety attack

If you feel one of these alarming attacks coming on, and if you have lavender growing in your garden or window box, put a handful of the flowers in a bowl along with 570 millilitres of cider vinegar and a few deep breaths of the fragrance will soon have you feeling relaxed again.

Athlete's foot – 1

Athlete's foot often succumbs to being treated with tea-tree oil diluted in suitable carrier oil, such as sweet almond oil. If you are scrupulous about drying between your toes, you reduce your chances of getting it considerably.

Athlete's foot – 2

If you rinse your affected foot (or feet) several times a day with cider vinegar, you will soon be fungus free. Always put on clean tights or socks after doing this and soak old ones in a solution of one part vinegar to five parts water before washing them.

Baggy eyes

If you have really baggy eyes, try gently rubbing some suppository cream into the offending area. The cream shrinks haemorrhoids and several Hollywood make-up artists swear that it does the same to eyebags. Give the cream a chance to settle before applying your usual maquillage. Others trust to holding an ice cube under each eye until it the cube melts.

Barbecue beauty

If you shower or bathe using coal tar soap before going to a summer's evening barbecue, you will keep annoying insects at bay.

Bathtime luxury

Add three or four tablespoonfuls of dried milk to your bathwater – much cheaper than using pint after pint of milk.

Bathtime safety

Always pull the plug out before getting out of the bath. Should you trip and fall back into the bath, knocking yourself out in the process, at least you won't drown!

Bedwetting

If your toddler is out of nappies but is still a bed wetter, try not giving him or her anything to drink for three hours before going to bed and just before you clean their teeth (or they go to clean their own teeth) give them a tablespoonful of honey. And if your youngster is going to stay overnight with a chum, tell the friend's mother about the problem and ask her to do the honey trick – it will save your youngster some embarrassment.

Blocked up nose

If your nose is blocked up fill a hot water bottle with really hot (but not boiling) water, add several drops of eucalyptus or camphor oil and tightly stopper it. When your nose bungs up, simply unscrew the stopper and inhale.

Blood donors

Next time you are scheduled to give blood, don't use handcream before you go. The chemicals the cream contains can affect the finger-prick test you have to have before actually giving your blood.

Blusher

Applying blusher can be difficult to get right, especially for beginners to the art of applying make-up. If you tilt your head downwards, the blood will run to your face, making it look as if you are blushing. Use the reddened areas as a guide and your blusher will look very natural.

Body lotion

Make expensive body lotions last twice as long by mixing them half-and-half with inexpensive, unperfumed body lotion. You won't notice any reduction in the strength of the scent and you'll save money, too.

Boils

Make a paste of flour and honey to apply to boils and abscesses. It will bring the boil to a head (and take the sting from the abscess).

Burned fingers

If you scald your fingers try grasping the lobe of your ear with them. The heat of the burn is absorbed by the ear – enough to take the pain from your fingers.

Buying perfume

Never buy a perfume you haven't worn before because you like the way it smells on you immediately. The initial aroma, or top notes, dry down to the middle notes and then to the base notes, which is the scent that lingers. Apply the tester as you would you normal perfume. If after an hour or two the dried-down scent still appeals, then buy it.

Caffeine substitute

Next time you need caffeine blast, aim for the fruit bowl and vegetable rack instead. Put some beetroot, apple and ginger in the juicer and drink that instead. Kick the caffeine habit and get into juicing for a few weeks and wait for people to tell you how great you look.

Chesty coughs

Put a sliced lemon and three cupfuls of water in a saucepan and bring to the boil. Add two tablespoonfuls of honey and two of glycerine. Stir well, remove the lemon and sip the elixir throughout the day.

Chocolate

Dark chocolate is an antioxidant and is better for you than milk chocolate.

Clothes shopping – 1

If you are off to the shops looking for a dress for a very special occasion, wear the underwear you plan to use on the big night and take the jewellery you will be using. And when you find the dress of your dreams, take it to the door to see it in the daylight rather than buy as soon as you've left the changing room.

Clothes shopping – 2

Next time you buy shoes, always set off for the shops in the morning – by the afternoon your feet will have swollen. And remember to wear tights.

Clothes shopping – 3

Buy one good cashmere sweater rather than two good merino wool ones. Buy one merino wool one rather than to two lambswool ones. In other words always buy one of the best you can afford rather than two of something else. Quality wins over quantity every time. With clever accessorizing you can wear the same basic garments time and time again.

Cold sores

As soon as you feel that slight tingle on your lips that heralds a cold sore, swamp a piece of gauze with witch hazel and dab it on the area. It often stops the sore developing, but if you are too late, repeat the witch hazel treatment, ignore the sting and the sore will soon dry out. Diluted white vinegar works, too.

Colds

If you feel a cold coming on, try and sneeze through your nose rather than with your mouth open.

Corns

Put a little wholemeal flour in a bowl and drizzle in a teaspoonful of vinegar to make a paste (you may need to add more flour to get a decent consistency). Spread this over the corn and press a thin slice of onion over it. Wrap a bandage round to keep everything in place and leave it there overnight.

Cramp – 1

If you suffer from cramp in the feet or legs at night, scrub any dirt off a medium-size potato and dry it thoroughly. Put it on your bed, somewhere you are not likely to disturb it as you move in your sleep, and you won't get cramp.

Cramp – 2

If you are feel sceptical going to bed with a potato (see above), try keeping a muslin bag containing corks in your bed. If you feel cramp coming on, holding a cork in a clenched fist keeps it at bay. And if you get cramp in your feet, put on a pair of loose bedsocks keeping a cork in place next to the usually affected spot will ease any cramp that threatens.

Cramp – 3

A syrup made up of a teaspoonful each of honey, cider vinegar and calcium lactate and taken by the teaspoon every few hours is a time-tested way of keeping cramp at bay.

Dentists

Never wait until you have toothache before making an appointment to go and see your dentist: by then it's too late. Have a regular check-up every six months. Many dentists send regular reminders: don't ignore them.

Detox

Detoxing can, but need not, mean drinking nothing but water and eating nothing but carrot juice for weeks on end. Try to have one day a week when you eat nothing but beautifully fresh, organic food and drink nothing but water and you will find that the boost to your system is out of all proportion to the effort involved.

Doctors appointments

In these days when you may have to wait several days for an appointment make notes of your symptoms – the sort of ache or pain you (or your child) has, when you have it (if it is intermittent) and how long each attack lasts. You may feel foolish reading from it when your doctor ask you what's wrong, but it's much more efficient than relying on your memory.

Dry hands

If you suffer from dry hands, try rubbing a good blob of handcream into them before you go to bed. When you wake up in the morning, you will be surprised at how soft they feel.

Dry lips

If your lips go dry in winter and the usual remedies don't work, try gently exfoliating them with an old, soft toothbrush for a minute or two then applying Vaseline or lip balm.

Ear infections

Despite the oft-repeated words, 'never put anything smaller than your elbow in your ear', a solution of equal parts of vinegar and olive oil applied to the ear with a cotton bud, often clears up ear infections.

Eyecare

If you spend hour after hour at the computer staring at the screen, buy the best pair of lightly tinted sunglasses you can afford and wear them from time to time when you are working. And if you wear glasses, ask your optician for a prescription for a pair of glasses with a hint of a tint – it's amazing how quickly your eyes will feel the benefit.

Eyelashes

If you don't like wearing mascara or are sensitive to it, ask your beautician to dye your eyelashes with a mild, vegetable dye. It will keep your lashes dark and lustrous for up to two months – and if you like the effect, have it done again.

Eyeliner

If your eyeliner is forever smudging, try dipping a wet brush in dark eye shadow and using this instead. It will stay unsmudged until you take it off at night.

Face powder

Loose powder sticks to moisturizers and cleansers and can look very heavy – with a correspondingly negative effect on the way you look. Avoid this by blotting your face with a tissue before you put any powder on. Always store your powder puff face towards the mirror in your compact as residual oil from your skin can affect the powder in your compact.

Face cloths

If you are one of those people who have no time in the morning for a lengthy beauty routine, when you are in the shower give your face a really good scrub with a clean facecloth and when you come out, put on some moisturizer. At night, use a clean facecloth to scrub your face again, and this time when you've finished rub in a little night cream.

Foundation

Tapping your foundation on to your face rather than blending it in gives much better coverage.

Fresh air

A pot plant kept at the side of a computer reduces the amount of carbon dioxide in the atmosphere and makes it less likely that you will feel like dropping off as you puzzle over your spreadsheets.

Fresh is best

Medical evidence suggests (and all doctors recommend) that we eat at least five helpings of fresh fruit and vegetables a day. And it's an easy recommendation to follow. A chopped up apple and an orange for breakfast (with some wheatgerm sprinkled on it), a salad for lunch and a banana on the drive home and that's it.

Fresh look

To keep your make-up looking as if it has just been applied, no matter how hot you feel, keep a small spray of water in your bag and give your face a light spray every so often. It will help you look great from morning till night.

Glow, Girl, Glow

If you are going to a party and you know you are the kind who 'shines' after a few dances in a hot room, make it look deliberate by wearing lip gloss and putting a sheen on your eyelids.

Hayfever

If you have mislaid or forgotten your usual hay-fever remedy, smear a little Vaseline inside each nostril. It should protect you from the worse effects of the pollen until you can get to your ante-histamines.

Head lice

Once thought to only affect other people's children, but now a sad fact of life for many mums of school-age youngsters, head lice can be kept at bay during a school epidemic by applying lavender essential oil to the child's hairline, behind the ears and at the nape of the neck. Do this as soon as you hear that lice are about, otherwise you will probably be too late.

Herbal baths

Put a selection of favourite-smelling herbs in the foot of a pair of tights and tie them to the bath tap after you have run your bath, so that they are immersed in the warm water. Then lie back and relax in your own herbal bath.

Hiatus hernia

If your life is blighted by a hiatus hernia, try eating a bowl of porridge before you go to bed each night. People who have done this swear that it soothes the pain and encourages a good night's sleep. (If you have high blood pressure, though, try and make the porridge without adding salt in the cooking.)

Hot flushes

If you suffer from hot flushes, try filling a rubber hot-water bottle three-quarters full with water and keeping it in the freezer. Next time you feel a flush coming on at home, held the bottle between the palm side of your wrists where the veins are quite prominent and you will cool down almost immediately. The same frozen hot-water bottle is also great for soothing hot feet.

Hungover?

One of the most pleasant ways of getting rid of hangover is to take six teaspoonfuls of honey every twenty minutes until you feel like a human being again. If you are feeling the effects of a heavy night, don't drive first thing next morning even after a few hours' sleep, you could still be unfit to drive.

Ice

An ice cube held against the bags under your eyes shrinks them temporarily. Try it before putting your make up on in the morning.

Indigestion

A syrup made up of a tablespoonful each of honey and vinegar and taken by the teaspoon followed by a glass of water when necessary is often all that is needed to settle a bout of indigestion.

In-flight exercise

When flying, no matter for how short a time, wiggle your toes, ankles and wrists vigorously every half an hour. Massage your calves and walk up and down the aisle at least once an hour.

Insect bites

Legion are the remedies for taking the sting out of insect bites, among them lavender essential oil (the only such oil that can be applied directly to the skin), vinegar (for wasp stings) and bicarbonate of soda (for bee stings). But perhaps the most curious are to apply toothpaste to the bite and, to soothe a wasp sting, hold the end of a red-tipped match against the affected area. They all work.

Instant face lift – 1

Fill a big basin with cold water and put your head under it. Blow bubbles for as long as you can and you will find when you resurface that your face feels fresher and tighter. This works all year round, but is especially good in summer.

Instant face lift – 2

Smile!

Instant relaxation

Next time you feel you're about to blow your top, find a quiet spot, take a deep breath through your nose, hold it for a count of ten and then breathe out through your mouth. Do this ten times and you should feel much more relaxed and in control of the situation.

Jet lag

Banish jet lag after long-haul flights by taking a supply of dried apricots with you. Refuse at least one of the meals and have the fruit instead. You will feel great when you arrive at your destination.

Jet-setting

When you fly off to foreign climes for your holiday, wear layers of smart, loose clothing and put a plastic coathanger in your hand-baggage. When you take off your top clothes, slip them on the hanger, smile nicely at the cabin crew and ask them if they can hang it somewhere for you. When you get off the plane you will look as smooth as your crease-free jacket.

Lipstick – 1

When you find a lipstick that you absolutely love, go back to the beauty counter and buy another six. Not only do some lipsticks go out of production, others may change subtly from batch to batch. What appears to be the most insignificant of changes in the tube may make it unsuitable for you on the lip.

Lipstick – 2

If your lipstick breaks, carefully repair it by melting the broken edges with a lighted match and gently press them together. Use a toothpick to smooth the edges and keep the lipstick in the fridge for a couple of hours.

Lipstick – 3

If you smooth a little foundation and a smidgen of translucent powder onto your lips before you put your lipstick on, it will last a lot longer. And if you don't have a tissue to blot it, a cigarette paper works just as well.

Mascara – 1

Next time you are putting your mascara on look directly into the mirror. Doing this makes it virtually impossible to get mascara in your eyes. And, unless you have sensitive eyes, try spraying just a little hairspray on to your mascara brush and applying it to your lashes. You won't have to worry about redoing your eyes for the rest of the day.

Mascara – 2

If your mascara is getting runny, leave the lid off overnight and it should dry out enough to make it usable. And if you think you have run out of mascara, stand the old one in cup of hot water for a minute or two. This loosens the very last bit of mascara and should give you enough for two more coats.

Medicine

If you are on regular medication that necessitates taking several tablets a day, find some clear glass bottles or jars, with airtight lids, and label them each a different day of the week. On a Sunday spend a few minutes transferring one day's medication into each bottle. Not only does this save time during the rest of the week when you are usually more rushed, but at a glance you can see if you have remembered to take your medication.

Model lips

For really professional, model-girl lips, apply your lipstick with a brush, following the contours of your lips, then define them with a lip pencil in an identical shade before blotting with a tissue. If you put your lipliner – cap on – in a glass of warm water for five minutes before applying it, you will get a perfect lip line.

Moisturizers

Don't use the same moisturizer all year round. In summer, especially when it's hot and humid, go for a lighter one than you wear in winter. And as most moisturizers last for about a year, when you go back to one after a break, check that the colour is the same as it was when you bought it. If it has changed, it's time to buy a new one.

Moisturizing

Everyone (even men) should cleanse, tone and moisturize their faces each day if they want a radiant skin. When you apply the moisturizer, avoid the eye area – the skin there is very delicate. Not only that, but women will coat their eyelashes with oil and their mascara will run.

Nails

If the tips of your nails are a work-a-day yellow or cream and you want them model-girl white, cut a lemon in half and push your nails into the flesh for a few minutes.

Nappy rash

A lightly beaten egg white spread over nappy rash clears it up a treat without there being any risk of baby suffering an allergic reaction to a shop-bought chemical cure.

Nailcare

Dripping your nails in warm olive oil mositurizes them, softens the cuticles and should stop them splitting. And if your nails tell the world that you are a heavy smoker, try cleaning them with minted toothpaste.

Nail varnish – 1

If you are in a rush to go out and your nail varnish hasn't dried, as long as it has been on for twenty minutes, you can run your nails under cold water to speed up the process. Nail varnish stays fresher for longer if you keep it in the fridge.

Nail varnish – 2

Keeping nail varnish in the fridge makes it last longer, and if you find that the top is always sticking, rub a little petroleum jelly on the top of the bottle. And remember that if your nail varnish bubbles, try rolling the bottle gently to even out the colour, rather than shaking it.

Nail varnish – 3

Using a colourless base before you apply your nail varnish stops nails discolouring. If you have short nails and want to make them look longer, go for dark shades and don't paint them right to the edge. Conversely, if you want to make small nails look bigger, go for metallic coloured nail varnish.

Nail varnish – 4

Some of the new fast-drying nail varnishes can make nails go yellow if you use them all the time. To prevent this happening, rub in some almond oil, give them a good buffing until they glow like pearls and give them a break from the nail varnish for a day or two.

Nail varnish – 5

If your hands are already a little sun-kissed and you want to make them look tanned, use a very pale purply-pink nail varnish.

Nerves

If you suffer from nerves, try taking a dessertspoon of ginseng elixir before you have breakfast and drink ginseng tea rather than your usual cuppa. During the day sip a glass of hot water with a teaspoon of honey, you will go to bed a much more relaxed person and wake up the next day fighting fit and raring to go.

Oatmeal bath

Put some oats in an old stocking, tie a knot in it and put it in the bath. The oats turn the water milky and moisturize your skin beautifully.

Oily blonde hair

Blondes of either sex who suffer from oily hair and who don't have time to wash it, can brush or comb some talcum powder through it for a quick fix.

Olive oil massage

Once every month, dip your finger in the best olive oil you have and very gently massage it into your face, neck and elbows. It moisturizes these areas thoroughly, deeply and beautifully.

Packing

When you pack to go on holiday, roll your clothes round tissue paper rather than fold them. Not only will they crease less, you can get more in your case. And always restrict what you pack to different shades of two colours: you can mix and match the entire holiday and everyone will think you have brought an endless supply of clothes with you.

Painting toenails

Painted toenails look great with sandals and flip-flops. Painted toes don't. Avoid getting paint on your toes by cutting an old sponge into small triangles and use them to keep the toes separate.

Perfume – 1

Spray a cloud of your favourite toilet water around the bedroom after you have dressed for the day, walk into it and you will smell beautifully for hours. And if you spray a little of your usual perfume on to your hairbrush before you brush your hair, you will find yourself more alluring than usual.

Perfume – 2

You know of course to apply perfume behind your ears, the temples, the nape of the neck, at the crook of the elbow and inside the wrists, but in summer when you are not wearing tights, try dabbing just a little behind the knees and on the elbows. Perfume rises and just a little at the pulse points there works wonders.

Perfume – 3

If you want your perfume to last all day, and you can afford it, buy *extrait de parfum*. It has the highest concentrates of the ingredients that give the perfume its scent and is more powerful than the more popular *parfum de toilette*, *eau de parfum* and *eau de toilette*. The *extrait* may be the most expensive, but a little goes a long way.

Perfume – 4

Avoid wearing perfume in the sun. Many contain oils that might cause brown spots to appear on the skin.

Pillow talk

If you are finding it hard to sleep, place a pot-pourri of dried herbs, lime blossom, hops, rosemary, lavender, jasmine and camomile – in a flat, linen 'envelope' and tuck it inside your pillow. The herbs, particularly the hops and lime blossom, have strong sleep-inducing properties and you will soon be sleeping soundly.

Puffy eyes

The morning after a big night out, dab a very small blob of eye gel around the eye, especially underneath as soon as you have washed your face. Leave it for a little while before using your usual moisturizer and then applying some concealer.

Redskin

If you have a reddish complexion, always use a foundation with a greenish tinge. When you put your make-up on over it, the red is neutralized and you will look much better.

Seasonal foods

Try to eat fruit and vegetables when they come into season. If you buy foods that are out of season, they will have been brought in from abroad or forced locally and will have lost a lot of their goodness in the process, no matter how well they are treated.

Shampooing

Have you noticed that all shampoo bottles exhort you to wash your hair once with the shampoo, rinse and repeat? A simple device to make you use twice as much shampoo as you need! Unless you hair is very dirty, one wash and rinse is enough. Any more and you are in danger of stripping your hair of natural oils.

Shining hair

For really soft, shining hair, use cold water for the final rinse and let it dry naturally, under a towel wrapped around your head. And when you come to brush it out, wrap a silk scarf round your hairbrush and use it to brush your hair.

Shingles

Do whatever your doctor orders and take whatever he or she prescribes, but if the itch still itches and the pain still hurts, try dabbing the affected area with undiluted vinegar several times a day.

Smooth complexion

For that special, smooth summer look mix a little moisturizer into your foundation. The difference is amazing.

Sore throat

Take an eggcupful of water, add two or three drops of lavender essential oil and a teaspoonful of vodka, gargle and spit out, and your sore throat will soon be but a memory.

Spot repair

If you have a really bad spot that ordinary make up will not disguise, why not use a dark eyeliner pencil to make it look like a beauty spot. Chances are no one will notice.

Spots and blemishes

Dab a little mudpack on a pimple or other occasional skin blemish before going to bed at night. By morning, the impurities should have been drawn out and you should be spot-free.

Stomach ache

Next time you or anyone in the family has a sore stomach try the cardamom remedy. Simple deseed a cardamom pod and chew the seeds with a large glass of water.

Storing cosmetics

Heat, light, air and moisture all have a damaging effect on cosmetics (especially perfumes) so keep them all in a cool, dark place and ensure that all containers are completely air- and watertight.

Sunburn

We all know that too much sun is bad for our skin and that we should always 'Slip and Slap' – slip on a T-shirt and slap on some high-protection-factor suncream before venturing out in strong sunshine. But we usually end up being sunburned at least once a summer. Next time it happens to you and you don't have any proprietary soothers, rub the affected area with freshly cut cucumber every couple of hours.

Suncare

A lightly tanned face is a great boost to the system – you look good and feel good. But exposing the skin to the sun is incredibly ageing. So when it's sunny, instead of your usual moisturizer, use a high protection factor sunscreen instead.

Sweaty palms

If you are embarrassed by sweaty palms, rub some antiperspirant into the palms before you go out. It should keep your hands dry all day.

Sweet breath

Keep one or two mint tea bags in your handbag or pocket and when you are on a dinner date and can't clean your teeth but want to make sure that your breath is sweet and fresh in anticipation of a goodnight kiss, ask for a cup of mint tea instead of coffee. If the restaurant doesn't serve it, ask for a cup of hot water and make your own.

Swimming tip

Swimming is great exercise – twenty minutes, three or four times a week and your heart will feel the benefit and you'll look great. So swimming is good for you – but it can be hell on the hair. If you swim every day in chlorinated or salt water, use shampoo one day and conditioner the next.

Teeth

Keep a toothbrush and a small tube of whitening toothpaste in your bag or office desk to clean your teeth after lunch and before you go straight out after work. And if you use a mouthwash, don't use one containing alcohol. They sometimes dry out the mouth and make the problem of bad breath even worse.

The time to eat

The old adage, 'Breakfast like a king, lunch like a prince and sup like a pauper,' is excellent advice. Eating a good, healthy breakfast gives you a great start to the day and keeps your energy levels up until lunchtime. A decent lunch keeps you going until supper. And eating a light supper allows your digestive system to cope with what you eat before going you go to bed at night.

Tights

Always keep at least one spare pair of tights (or stockings if that's your style) in your office desk. Ladders always seem to happen just when the boss calls you in to discuss something and you don't want to look like you don't care about the way you look.

Tired eyes

Everyone has their own favourite remedy for tired eyes, but one of the most effective and most popular is to put moistened camomile teabags on closed eyelids and keep them there for ten minutes.

To start the day

First thing in the morning sip a drink made from a squeezed lemon and boiling water. It cleanses the liver, gets your metabolism off to a flying start and is a great source of vitamin C. And if you want to give it some extra zest, try adding some chopped ginger.

Too much lipstick

You can test if you have overdone the lipstick by putting a finger very gently into the mouth and then even more gently pulling it out again. If there are any traces of lipstick on the finger, then you have put too much on.

Underwear

Silk is luxurious but expensive. Cotton is better by far – and cheaper. And never, ever wear knickers made of man-made fibre.

Unruly eyebrows

If, even after you have plucked them, your eyebrows are still all over the place, apply a little styling gel or mousse with an eyebrow brush.

Untangling hair

When untangling their hair after washing it, many people make the mistake of starting at the scalp and working towards the end. Wrong! Always start at the ends and work back towards the scalp

Warts

There are many suggested cures for warts, one of the oldest of old wife's tales being that if you bang them sharply with a Bible, they will vanish. One that has worked for even more people is to apply the juice of a dandelion stem three times a day until the wart goes. (Remember, if a wart changes in appearance, develops a crust or starts to bleed, see a doctor immediately – it could be malignant.)

Water, water everywhere

We all know we should, but how many of us actually swig the two litres of water doctors and beauty writers tell us are essential for our health and appearance? Why not establish a regime of sipping a glass of water on the hour every hour, from eight in the morning until three in the afternoon? It won't be long until you feel the benefit and look terrific, too. And while we're on the subject, in blind tasting after blind tasting, ordinary tap water beats expensive bottles of *aqua minerale* and *eau de source* more often than not.

Weekly treat

Give your feet a treat every week by indulging in a footbath. Pour some warm water into a suitable-size basin, sprinkle in some bath salts and a few drops of lavender or another favourite essential oil. Soak your feet for fifteen minutes, dry them with a thick, clean towel and rub in a little foot lotion. You will feel so much better. If you don't have quarter of an hour to do this, add a little peppermint essential oil to some sweet almond oil and rub it all over your feet.

With glass in hand

Next time you are at a party, finish each drink before filling your glass. That way you will know exactly how may glasses you have had and when it's time to stop. If you allow your host to keep topping up your glass, it's impossible to keep track on how much you are drinking – until it's too late.

Practical Household Hints

Laundry and needlework

Next time you are faced with a pile of laundry, just thank your lucky stars you live in the days of automatic washing machines, easy-care fabrics, washing powders that could bring a coal mine up sparkling white. Think of your poor grandmother who relied on soap and a washboard!

Angora

Untreated angora fibre is usually too soft and difficult to care for: that's why the angora jumpers you buy are usually mixed with other materials to strengthen them and make them easier to wash. Either hand wash it or put it in the machine on the wool cycle. Dry it flat and don't be tempted to hang it over a radiator when it's almost dry.

Averaging out

The instructions as to how much washing powder to use printed on the back of the packet are based on an average load weighing between two-and-a-half to three-and-a-half kilos of moderately dirty washing, so adjust the recommended quantity to suit your wash.

Blunt needles

Sharpen blunt needles by rubbing an emery board around the point. And if after doing that you are still having difficulty penetrating the fabric – especially heavy cloth – run a bar of soap over the needle before you start sewing, or push the point of the needle into some soap every so often as you work.

Bad stains

If you are using a heavy-duty detergent to attack a badly stained garment before consigning it to the washing machine, rub it in with a toothbrush or a small, clean paintbrush. It penetrates the material more effectively than rubbing it by hand.

Belts

If your child has outgrown a favourite belt (or if you have been overindulging and have put on a few pounds around the middle) take the buckle off, add a short end of narrow elastic to the buckle end then sew the buckle back in place.

Blouses

If you are making a new school blouse or shirt for your daughter, give it an extra-long tail. It will act as a petticoat under her skirt and help it keep its shape until she grows out of it.

Button up

If you are fed up having to untangle your washing when you take it out of the machine, try buttoning the sleeves of shirts and blouses to the front buttons. Unbutton them before you start the ironing.

Buttons – 1

When you're sewing on buttons, put a little clear nail varnish on the front and back of each button. It will stay on longer if the thread is sealed.

Buttons – 2

Before you get rid of old clothes cut the buttons, zips, hooks and eyes etc off and put them in your sewing box. You never know when they could come in handy. If you are giving your cast-offs to a charity shop, keep everything intact and in position.

Buttons – 3

Rather than using cotton to sew buttons onto heavy-duty clothing, use light fishing line instead. And if you are not an angler, dental floss is a good and just as long-lasting substitute.

Buttons – 4

String same-coloured, same-size buttons on dental floss with the ends tied together, on a large safety or hairpin with the ends twisted together. They all keep your sewing box tidy and save time rummaging through the usual box or tin of assorted, different-size buttons looking for the right one.

Boucle

The bobbly surface that boucle garments have is made up of loops and fibres that can become damaged if badly washed. Made from either cotton, wool or synthetic fabrics, wash it accordingly. If you are unsure, have it dry cleaned.

Brocade

Woven from several different fibres, some silk, some synthetic and with its raised surface, brocade is best left to the experts. Best take it to the dry cleaners!

Calico

Usually made from pure cotton, but sometimes mixed with synthetics, uncoloured calico feels a bit rough to the touch. Wash it as you would cotton, even if there is some synthetic in it, and if it needs to be whitened, add a drop of white spirit to the first wash.

Candlewick

Candlewick is usually made of cotton, but can sometimes contain synthetics. If you have such a bedspread wash candlewick according to the more delicate fabrics it contains. After you've dried it, you will need to restore the pile by giving it a good shake.

Canvas

Known for its strength and often used to make bags and deckchairs, if it needs to be cleaned wash it with detergent and warm water and scrub with a nail brush to remove any really stubborn stains

Cashmere

Although it's best to have cashmere garments dry-cleaned by specialists or hand wash them yourself, you can machine wash them. Put them in a net bag and wash them in the machine, using the delicate washing cycle. Once it's finished, rinse repeatedly to ensure that all the soap has gone, spin slowly and remove from the machine. Reshape and dry flat.

Cheesecloth

Lightweight and so loosely woven this fabric is somewhat impracticle for clothing. If you have any cheesecloth clothes, they have to be handwashed if they are to keep their shape. Don't wring them; use a towel to absorb the moisture and iron while still damp.

Chiffon

Floaty, lightweight chiffon. Just the thing for a romantic date on a warm, summer's evening. Unless it's made of synthetic material, have it dry-cleaned. If it's not made from silk, wash it according to the manufacturer's instructions. Iron it damp and ease the fabric back into shape as you go.

Cold water detergents

If you are ecologically-minded remember that cold water detergents are just as efficient as hot water ones, and they save on energy, too.

Colour-fastness

Always test if a fabric is colour-fast before you wash it for the first time. Do this by dampening a ball of cotton wool and leaving it for five minutes on a hem or another part that won't be seen. If any dye comes off, forget about machine-washing: either hand wash the garment very gently in cool water, or better still take it to the cleaners.

Conditioners

Fabric conditioners contain enzymes and coat clothes with traces of oil and/or metal. That's why they should never be used for nappies or for clothes that are worn with sensitive skins.

Corduroy

When you're working with corduroy or any fabric which has a nap, always mark the reverse side with an arrow made from masking tape, or stitch one with a tacking stitch (don't use chalk as it rubs off). When the nap runs upward the colour appears to be darker: when it's running downwards it seems to be lighter. The arrow will help you avoid making mistakes you'll have to unpick later.

Curtains

Every time you take your curtains down for washing or cleaning swap them to opposite ends of the window when you rehang them.

They will keep their colour more evenly if you do this.

Cutting thread

It's always easier to thread a needle if you cut the thread at an angle. Never break it or bite it. Trying to thread a needle that hasn't been cut properly can be really fiddly.

Darning – 1

You'll save yourself time if you darn a garment when a patch starts to thin rather than wait until a hole appears. And always start well outside the edges of the hole or worn patch.

Darning – 2

Always use a darning mushroom when darning unless you are mending a pair of gloves. In that case you should wear the glove on your non-sewing hand.

Delicates – 1

If you machine wash your more delicate clothes (hand washing is much kinder) put them in a pillowcase and tie the end with a cord before popping them into the washing machine.

Delicates – 2

Dry silk, chiffon and crepe garments between two towels to absorb the excess moisture then hang them on a hanger indoors to dry naturally. Never spin dry them.

Dirty collars

To get rid of these hard-to-shift rings of dirt on collars apply just a little washing-up liquid to them before washing them as usual.

Double strength

If you are sewing on buttons use a needle with an eye large enough to get doubled-up thread through. That way you stitch with four strands of thread and need fewer stitches to keep the button securely in position.

Drawers

If you rub the inside of wooden drawers with a lavender scented candle, your clothes smell nice and bugs will keep out.

Drying laundry

These days, when washing comes out of the machine more or less ready to iron, fewer and fewer people hang their laundry out to dry although freshly laundered sheets that have dried in the sun and breeze are one of the simplest pleasures of life. Having said that, do not dry nylon, wool or silk in the sun. Nylon looses its colour and sunshine weakens wool and silk.

Elasticated garments

Never wash elastic or elasticated garments in hot water or they will shrink. When you have washed them, don't wring or pull them – they'll stretch. After washing, spin them for a short time, rolled up in towel, to remove the excess moisture and dry them flat – like wool.

Embroidery

If you have a small piece of embroidery to work on, stretch the cloth over a suitably sized and clean metal fruit jar ring and keep it in place with a elastic band.

Fabric softener sheets

After you take your washing from the machine, keep used fabric softener sheets in a jar filled with liquid softener. When you are drying a load of clothes, take a sheet from the jar, squeeze out the excess moisture and bung it in the dryer.

Fabric softeners

Some fabric conditioners can cause greasy-looking stains on your washing, so remember to dilute them before adding to the wash. If it's too late, the stains usually succumb to a paste of water and detergent.

Flannel

You can wash flannel as you would wool, but best take it to the dry cleaners, especially if the garment being cleaned is a pair of once-white cricket flannels.

Fluff

Annoying bits of fluff, hair and dandruff can be removed from dark garments (any garment really but they show up most on dark garments) with a strip of Sellotape.

Hangers

If you find that some of your clothes slip off their hangers, wind thick elastic bands round and round both ends. That will keep the clothes on the hanger, not on the bottom of the wardrobe. And if you have plastic hangers, a couple of bits of Velcro attached to the top of the hanger will do the same trick.

Hanging clothes

Always hang the clothes you wear most well away from delicate ones that you put on for special occasions. If they are hung mixter-maxter, you may damage the delicates when you take the most-worn out and put them back in again.

Hard to match

If you can't find thread the exact shade of the cloth you are sewing, keep a reel of clear, monofilament thread in your sewing box. The colour of the cloth will come through and no one will ever know, as long as you stitch very, very carefully.

Hard water

If you live in a hard-water area, add a dessertspoon of bicarbonate of soda to the water when hand washing delicates. It softens the water.

Hems – 1

Dressmakers who don't have a dummy can still achieve even hems on long skirts by marking suitable lengths on an ordinary sink plunger. It stands up by itself and leaves your hands free to pin the hem to the required length.

Hems – 2

Another tip for dummyless dressmakers. Stretch a piece of string between the legs of a table and chair at the height off the ground the hem is to be. Rub the string with chalk, put on the skirt or dress and stand with it against the string. Turn slowly round, making sure that the fabric brushes against the string all the way round. The hem is marked all the way round.

Hems – 4

You don't have to stoop when marking the hem of a child's skirt if you ask the child to stand on a sturdy table while you pin or wield the French chalk. If you are measuring with a ruler, wind a rubber band round it at the height you want. Much easier on the eyes as you work around the hemline.

Hem creases

If you sponge a stubborn crease with some white vinegar and press it with a warm iron, it should disappear.

Instant patterns

If you keep flower- or bird-patterned fabric when you're recurtaining a room, cut the shapes out: you can use them to decorate plain-coloured curtains or cushion covers.

Instant repair

Patch the knees of worn jeans by gluing on an appropriate-sized adhesive patch. It saves tedious sewing time. But if you are thinking of doing this on your children's jeans (especially teenage children) ask first if they want their jeans patched. Sometimes it is fashionable to have ripped, worn jeans.

Instructions

Write clear instructions on how to operate the washing machine on a piece of white card, put it inside a clear plastic wallet and tape it on top of, on the door of, or on the wall alongside the machine.

Ironing – 1

As soon as the children are old enough, get them to iron their own things or let them go to school with their clothes creased.

Ironing – 2

Dampen dry clothes with a plant spray before ironing them.

Ironing – 3

Leave the iron for about five minutes after switching it on before using it. Some thermostats take time to settle, and if you use your iron right away, it may be hotter than you want. And always start with items that require cool ironing. Adjusting the thermostat upwards and then ironing, is safer than adjusting it downwards.

Ironing buttons

If the buttons on a favourite blouse are very delicate, cover them with the bowl of a spoon when ironing round them.

Ironing handkerchiefs

Iron cotton handkerchiefs (and dish towels) three layers thick.

Ironing sheets

Why bother? They're just going to get crumpled! But if you insist, fold them first. It cuts the ironing time in half.

Irons – 1

Clean the plate of your iron by rubbing it while still hot over a piece of rough damp cloth stretched tight over the ironing board.

Irons – 2

Never wrap the flex round the iron while it is still hot – you could damage the flex. If the flex is in the least bit worn, have it replaced professionally.

Knits

If your knitted clothes come out of the wash covered with lots of little balls of fluff, stroke them very gently with a safety razor.

Knitting – 1

Knitters who are following a pattern that demands that some stitches be slipped off the needles can stop them dropping by threading a pipe-cleaner through them. Bend the ends under the stitches and they will be safe until they are picked up again.

Knitting – 2

To make it easier to count the stitches, use dark needles when working with light wool and white ones if the wool you are using is dark.

Knitting – 3

You can reuse wool if you wind it tightly round a piece of cardboard or wood, dip it in lukewarm water for a minute or two and let it dry naturally. All the kinks come out and it is ready to use again.

Knitting – 4

If you don't have a tape measure use nail varnish to mark inches or centimetres on one of the needles.

Knitting – 5

If you put your needles down for a moment, clamp them together with a large spring clothes peg. It stops the stitches dropping off and the knitting unravelling.

Laundry baskets

Assign each member of the family their own colour laundry basket and as you iron put each item in whomsoever's basket it belongs. If they won't help with the ironing, at least they can put their own clothes away.

Lace

Modern, machine-made lace is often tough especially if it is made of synthetic fibre. If you are laundering old, delicate hand-made lace wash it inside a white pillow case or cloth bag. And it's best pressed under a cloth, thus removing the danger of catching the fronds under the iron. If it is very old and very delicate, pin the lace flat on a linen-covered board (making sure that the pins you use won't rust) then sponge the lace clean with soapy water. Leave it to dry on the board.

Lingerie

Slip the stoppers from empty perfume bottles under the lining paper in your lingerie drawer. The traces of perfume on the stopper will keep your lingerie smelling sweet for ages.

Measuring tapes

Iron a limp measuring tape between two sheets of waxed paper, it will add a few months to its life and make it much easier to use.

Mohair

If you have washed a mohair jumper and it's a bit flat, restore its fluffiness by gently rubbing a strip of Velcro over it.

Napkins

Don't throw an old, worn tablecloth out. There's certain to be enough material there to make at least six napkins from it. And if you machine-stitch the hem with a contrasting colour thread, they will make a welcome addition to your dinner table.

Needles

If your needles are getting blunt and the budget is very, very tight thread them and run them through a piece of sandpaper. Best wear a pair of gloves when doing this, just in case you rub your skin along the abrasive paper.

New pillowcases

If you cut the backs off two old shirts and stitch them together down the long sides and along one of the short ones you have perfectly serviceable pillowcases.

No cuts

If you are cutting a button off, slide a comb under the button and cut the thread above the comb, very carefully with a razor.

Old dresses

If you have a favourite dress that is worn in the skirt and not the bodice, or vice versa, why not cut the unworn top off and turn it into a skirt, or discard the worn skirt and make a blouse out of the bodice?

Old slips

Old half-slips that still have wear in them, but which you no longer wear, make excellent lining for woollen skirts, which, if they are not lined, quickly loose their shape. Simply cut out the elastic waistband and stitch it in place.

Out of harm's reach

If you have young children and you keep your detergents and washing powders at the bottom of the cupboard under the sink, don't. Nearly all laundry products are at least mildly toxic – at worst seriously poisonous. So keep them where little hands can't get at them.

Patchwork

For an instant family heirloom, scour charity shops for suitable old clothes, cut them into usable squares and you have the essentials to make a fabulous patchwork quilt or throw.

Plastic

When next you are using your sewing machine to sew plastic put it between two sheets of greaseproof paper. If you do this, it won't stick, and after the job is finished, simply rip the paper away leaving the stitching intact.

Pins and needles

If you drop pins and needles on the floor, don't even think about trying to pick them up in your hands. Simply reach into your sewing box for the magnet you keep there and pick them up that way.

Pockets

Always turn out pockets and brush them free of all dirt and dust before washing a garment. Not only does this prevent accidental staining and protect garments (and the machine) from damage from foreign objects, you never know: you could come across a fiver that you thrust into your pocket and have completely forgotten about.

Pollen stains

Yellow lilies look lovely but they can stain your clothes if you rub against them. Either soak the stained item in a bowl of cold water and leave it in the sunlight or lay a piece of Sellotape over the marks. When you take it off, the marks should come away, too.

Pyjamas

Before you put pyjama bottoms or draw-string pants into the machine, tie the ends of the cord together so it doesn't slip out in the wash.

Save shrinkage

Always read the label before you put anything in the washing machine!

Sewing machine – 1

The best way to clean fluff from the working parts of a sewing machine is to use a pastry brush.

Sewing machine – 2

When you are using your machine, Sellotape a paper bag to the side of your sewing table (if it's a highly polished family heirloom, best fix the weight with a weight). As you work you can sweep fabric scraps and bits of thread into it and you will save on the cleaning up when you have finished.

Sewing machine – 3

Threading a sewing machine needle can be a bind. Slip a piece of white paper under the foot of the machine and the eye of the needle shows up much more clearly.

Sewing machine – 4

A piece of foam rubber fixed on the underside of the foot pedal of your sewing machine stops it moving across the floor as you work.

Sewing machine – 5

Fix a tape measure along the front edge of your sewing machine with double-sided tape and you won't have to waste time wondering where the heck you put it when you are at your machine and need to measure something.

Sewing plastic

If you find that your needle sticks when you are sewing plastic fabric, dust some talcum powder onto the needle before you start.

Sewing sheets

Save on new sheets by cutting sheets that are starting to wear in the middle in half then turning the sides to centre and stitching them together. New sheets from old.

Shiny trousers

If the seat of your pants has become shiny, dip a flannel in turpentine and rub it over the shiny bits.

Shortening trousers

Unless you are an expert, have this done by a tailor. Shortened trousers are difficult to get hanging correctly again. But if you are determined to master the art, practise on one or two old pairs first.

Silk ties

If you have any silk ties that look a little tired, try hanging them in a steamy bathroom or wrapping a piece of damp cloth round the plate of your iron and run the steaming iron over the tie.

Skirts

To lengthen a skirt add a band of either contrasting or matching material round the hem and add a bow or some other sort of decoration.

Slippery fabrics

If you find that shiny fabrics slip all over the table when you are stitching them on the machine, stretch a piece of towelling over the tabletop. The towel surface will keep the fabric where you want it. Also, when seaming slippery fabrics, put a piece of paper underneath them, The paper will keep the cloth in place and can be ripped off when you have finished sewing.

Snarled thread

If you find that the thread you are using is forever snarling, try rubbing fabric softener, beeswax, soap or paraffin along it.

Starch

Never starch anything except cotton or linen. When you do starch something, do so in a bowl, not the washing machine. Spin it dry afterwards but remember to rinse the machine afterwards to get rid of the starch deposits.

Steam irons

Try to avoid using tap water to fill your steam iron; it furs up the inside eventually. You can buy distilled water from a hardware shop (not a garage: the distilled water available in garages sometimes contains acid), but defrosted water from your freezer or water that has been boiled in a kettle is almost as good.

Stuffing

If you enjoy soft-toy making as a hobby, cut up pieces of about-to-be-discarded knitwear or old tights make excellent stuffing. You can use them to stuff cushions that are becoming a bit saggy, too.

Synthetic thread

If you are using synthetic thread, you may find that static electricity makes the thread stick to the garment. You can get round this by keeping the thread in the refrigerator for a few hours before you start sewing. It collects humidity and this reduces the clinging.

Thimbles

Always wear a thimble on your middle finger when sewing – it makes the task much easier and less painful. And if it is too loose, put a small, fabric Elastoplast on your fingertip and put the thimble over it.

Threading needles – 1

Buy a needle threader from your haberdasher. It will save hours of frustration as you try to get the thread through the eye of the needle.

Threading needles – 2

If, having tried, tried and tried again, you still can't thread a needle and you don't have a threader (see above), dip the end of the thread into clear nail varnish or spray some hairspray onto it. Stiff, the thread should be much easier to control.

Tidy reels

If your sewing box is a jumble of loose ends of thread, put a rubber band round the reel and tuck the loose end in, or you can keep it in place with a piece of sticky tape. Another way is to stick a drawing pin into the top of the reel and wind the loose end round that. Whichever you choose, your sewing box will be a lot tidier.

Tight sweater

If a favourite jumper has become too tight transform it into a cardigan. Measure the exact centre of the front and stitch down either side. Slit between the stitched lines and decorate the edges with ribbon. You can, if you like, make buttonholes and stitch on buttons, but you don't need to.

Tight waistband

If you have put on enough weight to make the wasitbands on trousers and skirts just a little tight, replace the thread on any buttons on the waistband with elasticated thread. You'll find them much more comfortable to wear as you diet to take the extra pounds off.

Tights

If you are constantly ripping your tights you may find that if you keep them in the freezer, they last much longer because doing so strengthens them. You can also avoid rips when putting stockings on by wearing cotton gloves when putting them on.

Washing gloves

Put the gloves on, wash your hands, and then stuff them (the gloves) with newspaper to dry them.

Washing wool

Before you machine-wash a knitted sweater or any woollen garment, turn it inside out. It helps to prevent wear and fading. You should do the same with anything quilted or made of perma-press material, too.

White towels

If your white towels are a bit grey but still have life in them –
dye them.

Woollens

When selecting the wool to darn or repair an woollen garment,
chose one that matches not just the colour, but also the weight of
the wool.

Zips – 1

Zips won't stick if you rub them with the edge of a bar of soap.
Rubbing them with a pencil often does the trick, too.

Zips – 2

To repair a zip that's broken near the bottom, pull the slide down to
below where the teeth have come adrift, then very carefully pull the
tab up, above the gap, making sure the gap matches on both sides.
Stitch them together just above the break and the zip will work
until you get round to fitting a new one.

Zips – 3

If the tab comes off a zipper, fix a small paperclip through the
aperture and wind suitably coloured thread round it. No one
will notice.